SACRED
HOOPS

PHIL JACKSON AND HUGH DELEHANTY

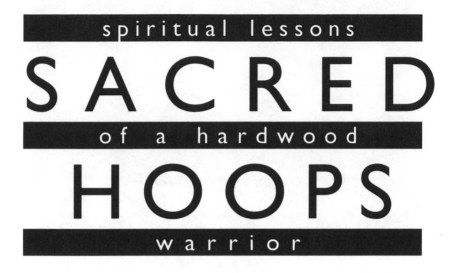

spiritual lessons

SACRED

of a hardwood

HOOPS

warrior

FOREWORD BY SENATOR BILL BRADLEY

HYPERION   NEW YORK

Library of Congress Cataloging-in-Publication Data

Jackson, Phil.
    Sacred hoops : spiritual lessons of a hardwood warrior /
by Phil Jackson and Hugh Delehanty.—1st ed.
        p.   cm.
    ISBN 0-7868-6206-8
    1. Jackson, Phil. 2. Basketball coaches—United States—Biography. 3. Chicago Bulls (Basketball team) I. Delehanty, Hugh, 1949– . II. Title.
    GV884.J32A3   1995
    796.323′092—dc20
    [B]   95–34543
                                                                            CIP

First Edition

10   9   8   7   6   5   4   3   2   1

For June and Barbara,
without whose love and selflessness
this book could never have been written

In memory of Eddie Mast, a teammate and a soulmate

The bull is the eternal principle of life, truth in action.
—KAKUAN (12TH CENT.),
In Nyogen Senzaki and Paul Reps,
Zen Flesh, Zen Bones

It is not the same to talk of bulls as to be in the bullring.
—SPANISH PROVERB

CONTENTS

FOREWORD

For two years on the road with the New York Knicks, I roomed with Phil Jackson. It was in this setting that I came to understand the depth, compassion, competitiveness, and strength of this tall man from North Dakota.

Finely shaped by his parents' religious experience, the vast openness of the upper plains, and a game he loved, Phil reached the ultimate, the NBA World Championship, five times—twice as a player and three times as a coach. His experience as a player, surrounded by the hype and attention afforded to athletes in New York City, prepared him for coaching the Bulls at a time when Chicago became the basketball capital of the world.

People often ask me if I ever thought Phil Jackson would make a good coach. No question about it. The ingredients were there even in his playing days. He was always analytical in his assessment of players and the game. He was committed to learning, to teaching, and to acting on his insights. He understood that winning meant giving up something small for yourself so that the team could gain. Finally, he was astute enough to understand that in order to win, you needed a strategy both on the court and off.

Here's another comment I have heard: "Anybody can coach a team led by Michael Jordan to the World Championship." This comment signifies both an unfamiliarity with Phil Jackson and with the game of basketball. Of course, it is true that Michael Jordan can do things on the court that no one else has ever approached. The Bulls, though, are a team, and not just one player. They won their three championships, without either a dominant center or an all-star point guard, because all of the players worked together toward the same goal, sacrificing themselves for the betterment of the team.

Getting players to this level, though, was not easy. Phil's most difficult obstacle to overcome was the relationship between Michael Jordan and the rest of his teammates. When Phil first took over the Bulls in 1989, many of his players had a tendency to stand around and admire Michael Jordan and his creativity, which limited their impact as a team. Phil changed that. He knew that a player is only one point on a five-pointed star. Oscar Robertson once told me that the really great player takes the worst player on his team and makes him good. Phil convinced Michael that that was the route to his true greatness and the only path to reaching the championship—the prize that surpasses individual stardom.

As I watched the Chicago championship teams I could not help but be reminded of the Knicks of the early 1970s. Indeed, the similarities are striking—strong ball movement, tough defense, always finding the open man, and always seizing on opposing teams' offensive or defensive weaknesses. In the transformation of the Bulls from championship contenders to champions, Phil emphasized foremost tough defense and passing skills. It was teamwork in its purest form, and it was vintage Knick basketball from the championship year.

In *Sacred Hoops, Spiritual Lessons of a Hardwood Warrior*, Phil opens up his chest of secrets and shares them with his readers. As you read of Phil's experiences in professional basketball, from New York City to Albany, Puerto Rico, and finally Chicago, I know you will find this book as entertaining and educational as I did. Phil has learned his lessons well, from Red Holzman with the Knicks, Bill Fitch at the University of North Dakota, and from the memorable Zen Master. I'm sure when you finish reading this book, you'll see that Phil Jackson does not fit any stereotypes. He's a thinker, a compassionate man, a passionate man, and most important, a leader from whom there is much to learn.

—SENATOR BILL BRADLEY

SACRED
HOOPS

INTRODUCTION

This is a book about a vision and a dream. When I was named head coach of the Chicago Bulls in 1989, my dream was not just to win championships, but to do it in a way that wove together my two greatest passions: basketball and spiritual exploration.

On the surface this may sound like a crazy idea, but intuitively I sensed that there was a link between spirit and sport. Besides, winning at *any* cost didn't interest me. From my years as a member of the championship New York Knicks, I'd already learned that winning is ephemeral. Yes, victory is sweet, but it doesn't necessarily make life any easier the next season or even the next day. After the cheering crowds disperse and the last bottle of champagne is drained, you have to return to the battlefield and start all over again.

In basketball—as in life—true joy comes from being fully present in each and every moment, not just when things are going your way. Of course, it's no accident that things are more likely to go your way when you stop worrying about whether you're going to win or lose and focus your full attention on what's happening *right this moment*. The day I took over the Bulls, I vowed to create an environment based on the principles of selflessness and compassion I'd learned as a Christian in my parents' home; sitting on a cushion practicing Zen; and studying the teachings of the Lakota Sioux. I knew that the only way to win consistently was to give everybody—from the stars to the number 12 player on the bench—a vital role on the team, and inspire them to be acutely aware of what was happening, even when the spotlight was on somebody else. More than anything, I wanted to build a team that would blend individual talent with a heightened group consciousness. A team that could win big without becoming small in the process.

Before joining the Bulls' coaching staff in 1987, I was ready to say goodbye to basketball and let my 20-year career in the sport become history. Over the years I'd grown disenchanted with the way power, money, and self-glorification had tainted the game I love. I'd recently left a head coaching job in the Continental Basketball Association, frustrated by how shamelessly ego-driven the game had become, and determined to find something else to do with my life. I was contemplating returning to graduate school when Jerry Krause, the Bulls' vice president of basketball operations, called and offered me a job as an assistant coach.

The more I learned about the Bulls, the more intrigued I

became. It would be like going to "graduate school in basketball," I told my wife, June. The coaching staff included a couple of the best minds in the game: Johnny Bach, a man with an encyclopedic knowledge of basketball, and Tex Winter, the innovator of the famed triangle offense, a system that emphasizes cooperation and freedom, the very values I'd spent my life pursuing off the court and dreamed of applying to the game. What's more, the team also had the most creative player in basketball—Michael Jordan. I "was excited" to give basketball another chance.

It was the best decision I ever made.

Most leaders tend to view teamwork as a social engineering problem: take x group, add y motivational technique and get z result. But working with the Bulls I've learned that the most effective way to forge a winning team is to call on the players' need to connect with something larger than themselves. Even for those who don't consider themselves "spiritual" in a conventional sense, creating a successful team—whether it's an NBA champion or a record-setting sales force—is essentially a spiritual act. It requires the individuals involved to surrender their self-interest for the greater good so that the whole adds up to more than the sum of its parts.

This isn't always an easy task in a society where the celebration of ego is the number one national pastime. Nowhere is this more true than in the hothouse atmosphere of professional sports. Yet even in this highly competitive world, I've discovered that when you free players to use *all* their resources—mental, physical, and spiritual—an interesting shift in awareness occurs. When players practice what is known as mindfulness—simply paying attention to what's actually happening—not only do they play better and win more, they also become more attuned with each other. And the joy they experience working in harmony is a powerful motivating force that comes from deep within, not from some frenzied coach pacing along the sidelines, shouting obscenities into the air.

No team understood better than the championship Chicago Bulls that selflessness is the soul of teamwork. The conventional wisdom is that the team was primarily a one-man show—Michael Jordan and the Jordanaires. But the real reason the Bulls won three straight NBA championships from 1991 to '93 was that we plugged in to the power of *oneness* instead of the power of one man, and transcended the divisive forces of the ego that have crippled far more gifted teams. Center Bill Cartwright said it best: "Most teams have guys who want to win, but aren't willing to do what it takes. What it takes is to give yourself over to the team and play your part. That may not always make you happy, but you've got to do it. Because when you do, that's when you win."

When Jordan came out of retirement and returned to the Bulls in the spring of 1995, expectations rose in a deafening crescendo. Michael Jordan is the greatest athlete on the planet—the argument went—then, *ipso facto*, the Bulls should win the championship. Even some of the players, who should have known better, bought into this line of reasoning. But what happened instead was that the team lost the identity it had forged in Jordan's absence and regressed to the way it had been in the late eighties when the players were so mesmerized by his moves that they played as if they were mere spectators at the show.

To succeed, the new Bulls will have to rediscover the selfless approach to competition that inspired their predecessors. They will have to expand their minds and embrace a vision in which the group imperative takes precedence over individual glory, and success comes from being awake, aware, and in tune with others.

That lesson is important in all areas of life, not just on the basketball court. My friend and former assistant coach Charley Rosen used to say that basketball is a metaphor for life. He applied basketball jargon to everything he did: if someone paid him a compliment, he'd say, "nice assist"; if a taxicab nearly mowed him down, he'd shout, "great pick." It was an amusing game. But, for me, basketball is an expression of life, a single, sometimes glittering thread, that reflects the whole. Like life, basketball is messy and unpredictable. It has its way with you, no matter how hard you try to control it. The trick is to experience each moment with a clear mind and open heart. When you do that, the game—and life—will take care of itself.

chapter ONE

THE SECOND

COMING

*The best way to make your dreams
come true is to wake up.*
—PAUL VALERY

The team room at the Sheri L. Berto Center is the perfect setting for an epiphany. It's the inner sanctum of the Chicago Bulls—a sacred space adorned with Native American totems and other symbolic objects I've collected over the years. On one wall hangs a wooden arrow with a tobacco pouch tied to it—the Lakota Sioux symbol of prayer—and on another a bear claw necklace, which, I'm told, conveys power and wisdom upon its beholder. The room also contains the middle feather of an owl (for balance and harmony); a painting that tells the story of the great mystical warrior, Crazy Horse; and photos of a white buffalo calf born in Wisconsin. To the Sioux, the white buffalo is the most sacred of animals, a symbol of prosperity and good fortune.

I had the room decorated this way to reinforce in the players' minds that our journey together each year, from the start of training camp to the last whistle in the playoffs, is a sacred quest. This is our holy sanctuary, the place where the players and the coaches come together and prepare our hearts and minds for battle, hidden from the probing eyes of the media and the harsh realities of the outside world. This is the room where the spirit of the team takes form.

Early in the morning on March 7, 1995, I held an informal meeting in the team room with assistant coaches Tex Winter and Jimmy Rodgers to review some game tapes and discuss what to do with the team. Even though Scottie Pippen was having an MVP-caliber season and Toni Kukoc had begun to flower, the team had developed a disturbing tendency to build up huge double-digit leads in the first half, only to fall apart in the closing minutes of the game. Part of the problem was that we had lost two important big men in the off-season: Horace Grant, an All-Star power forward who had signed on as a free agent with the Orlando Magic, and Scott Williams, who had jumped to the Philadelphia 76ers. As a stopgap measure, we were playing Kukoc at power forward, but though he gave it a gallant try, he wasn't strong or aggressive enough to fend off bruisers like Charles Barkley and Karl Malone.

During the All-Star break in February, I had met with owner Jerry Reinsdorf in Phoenix to discuss the future of the team. In the year and a half since we had won our last NBA title, we had lost all but three of the regulars on our championship teams, including Bill Cartwright, now with the Seattle Supersonics; John Paxson, the Bulls' newest radio announcer, and Michael Jordan, who had retired in 1993 and was playing for Reinsdorf's other organization, the Chicago White Sox. Reinsdorf was convinced that unless the Bulls had a strong infusion of new talent, we would probably languish around the .500 mark for years. He was considering trading some veterans—notably Pippen—for young stars in order to rebuild the franchise. He asked me if I would be willing to stick with the team through what could be a long, sometimes frustrating process of renewal. I told him I would.

Secretly I hoped that we could find another solution. I was dubious that we could ever get fair value for Pippen, easily the best all-around player in the league, and I was relieved when the trading deadline passed in late February and Scottie was still on the team. What the Bulls needed wasn't something a quick trade could provide; the team needed that unshakable desire to win that Cartwright, Paxson, and, most of all, Jordan had in their bones. How could you trade for that? As I mulled these problems over in the team room with Tex and Jimmy, I tried to put an optimistic spin on the situation. But deep inside, I sensed that the players had already surrendered. They had grown comfortable with the idea of being a .500 team.

Then Michael Jordan walked in the door.

Dressed in a dark warmup suit, he glided into the room and took a seat in the back as if he had never left.

A couple of days earlier he had walked out of the White Sox spring training camp in Sarasota, Florida, and returned to Chicago, to avoid becoming a pawn in the baseball strike. Michael was adamant about not crossing the picket line, so he packed his bags rather than play in the exhibition season, which was starting that week.

"What's going on?" I asked him. "Are you ready to suit up?"

He smiled and said, "It looks like baseball isn't going to happen for me."

"Well," I replied, "I think we've got a uniform around here that might fit you."

Michael and I had joked before about a possible comeback, but this time I could tell it wasn't just banter. In September, before the team officially retired his number in a made-for-TV ceremony at our new arena, the United Center, I told him I thought he was jumping the gun. There was no reason why a superbly conditioned athlete like Michael, who was then only thirty-one, couldn't return to the game and play into his late thirties. He said he was participating in the ceremony as a favor to Jerry Reinsdorf and to raise money for a youth center on the west side of Chicago named in honor of his father, James Jordan, who had been brutally murdered the year before.

"What if the strike doesn't get settled?" I had asked him that day. "What if your whole year gets blown out of the water?"

"That's a possibility," he'd replied. "But I don't think that's going to happen."

"Well, if it does happen, you could come back here and play basketball. All you'd need is twenty-five games or so to get ready for the playoffs. We could use you down the stretch."

"Twenty-five—that's too many."

"Okay, maybe twenty."

I knew then that he would consider coming back if Major League Baseball couldn't get its act together by spring training. Which it didn't—and that's why he had returned to the Berto Center. When we were alone, Michael asked if he could come to practice the next day and work out with the team to see how it felt to have a basketball in his hands again.

Knowing Michael, a little sweat and intense competition was all he needed to make up his mind.

THAT OLD-TIME RELIGION

None of us could have predicted what was going to happen next. The effect on the team, from the very first practice, was electric. The players—most of whom had never played with Michael before—were thrilled about the prospect of his return, and the level of competition at practice rose instantly. Even though he wasn't in game shape, Michael challenged everybody to step up. Scottie Pippen and B. J. Armstrong, who had felt burdened by the team's inconsistent performance, suddenly came alive, and Toni Kukoc was almost giddy with excitement. Even Pete Myers, the player who stood to lose his spot in the starting lineup, was excited.

What Michael brought to the team was not only his extraordinary talent, but a deep understanding of the system of basketball we played. He was versatile enough to play all five positions on the floor, and could show by example how the system worked at its most sophisticated level. This was extremely valuable for the newcomers to the team. Before practice, I often found Michael working out, one-on-one, with young players like Corie Blount and Dickey Simpkins. It reminded me of the days when a younger Pippen and Jordan would work on dunking left-handed or making a 180° spin move from the corner.

Over the next two weeks, while Michael was deciding what to do with his life, the team transformed before our eyes, invigorated by Jordan's presence on the practice floor. We won the next four out of five games, including a dramatic victory over Cleveland, one of the most physically intimidating teams in the league, and a last-minute come-from-behind win over Milwaukee. The Indiana Pacers' coach Larry Brown predicted that with Jordan in the lineup the Bulls would be the favorites to win the NBA championship. I didn't think that was a realistic assessment of the situation, but maybe I was wrong. Perhaps Michael could perform a miracle.

The whole world seemed to be swept up in the myth of Michael Jordan, superhero. As he started working out with the team, the word spread, and on his second day of practice, an army of reporters, photographers, and TV crews from all over the globe began to swell outside the Berto Center. One morning I saw a swarm of media descend on Scottie Pippen's car as he entered the parking lot, hoping that he might open his window and throw them a few crumbs of information. At the front of the line was sportscaster Dick Schaap, and I realized this must be a pretty big story.

I tried to protect Michael as much as I could. I'd let him leave the floor early so that when the reporters came rushing on court after practice, he'd already be gone. Early on I asked him how long it was going to take him to make his decision, and he said about a week and a half. So I told the reporters that they should go home and come back in a week or so when we had something to tell them. What a mistake! After that they attacked the story as if it were the O. J. Simpson trial.

What interested me was the religious overtone to the proceedings. Perhaps it was the fact that the nation had spent the last year caught up in the O.J. case, suffering the disillusionment of watching a one-time beloved sports great being tried for the murder of his ex-wife and her friend. Perhaps it was just a reflection of the spiritual malaise in the culture and the deep yearning for a mythic hero who could set us free. Whatever the reason, during his hiatus from the team, Michael had somehow been transformed in the public mind from a great athlete to a sports deity.

The Associated Press reported that, in a survey of African-American children, Jordan had tied with God as the person they most admired after their parents. A radio station in Chicago asked listeners if Jordan should be named king of the world, and 41 percent of the respondents said yes. And fans were spotted kneeling and praying at the foot of Jordan's statue in front of the United Center. To poke fun at the media's adoration of Jordan, Tim Hallam, the Bulls' wry director of media services, started referring to him and his entourage as Jesus and the Apostles. "Jesus goes to the bathroom," Hallam would announce in a mock broadcaster's baritone. "Details at eleven."

THE MYTH OF THE SUPERHERO

Michael found the whole thing a little embarrassing. I've always been impressed by his ability to remain humble and down to earth despite all the attention he receives. But the hysteria surrounding his comeback created a division between Michael and his teammates that ultimately had an adverse effect on the team. The new players, which included everyone except Armstrong, Pippen, and Will Perdue, never got to know Michael intimately, nor he them—and that eventually undermined the team's performance on court. Basketball is a sport that involves the subtle interweaving of players at full speed to the point where they are thinking and moving as one. To do that successfully, they need to trust each other on a deep level and know instinctively how their teammates will respond in pressure situations. A great player can only do so much on his own—no matter how breathtaking his one-on-one moves. If he is out of sync psychologically with everyone else, the team will never achieve the harmony needed to win a championship.

There's a passage from Rudyard Kipling's *Second Jungle Book* that I often read during the playoffs to remind the team of this basic principle:

> *Now this is the Law of the Jungle—*
> *as old and as true as the sky;*
> *And the Wolf that shall keep it may prosper,*
> *but the Wolf that shall break it must die.*
> *As the creeper that girdles the tree trunk,*
> *the Law runneth forward and back—*
> *For the strength of the Pack is the Wolf,*
> *and the strength of the Wolf is the Pack.*

Before Michael arrived, the Bulls were beginning to gel as a team. The main thing we needed, I thought, was to strengthen our resilience in the fourth quarter—and that's what Jordan was famous for. What I didn't anticipate was the impact Jordan's presence would have on the psyche of the team. I was so busy focusing on protecting Michael's privacy, I lost sight of how isolated he was from his teammates and what that was doing to the other players.

Kukoc was simply awestruck. A talented forward from Croatia whom Jerry Krause considers the best pure passer since Magic Johnson, Toni was devastated in 1993 when Jordan announced his retirement, only a few days after Kukoc had joined the team.

Now he was finally getting a chance to play with Jordan, and he was so intimidated he refused to go one-on-one against him in practice. Even when we'd run a special play for Toni that called for him to drive to the basket, he'd pull up and take a short jumper instead.

Once Michael officially joined the team and started playing in games, the situation didn't improve. Some of the players were so bedazzled by his moves they'd unconsciously step back and wait to see what he was going to do next. And Michael was so absorbed in his struggle to prove to himself that he still had the touch, he often made uncharacteristic misjudgments. To make matters worse, his teammates were reluctant to make demands on him. In one game, Michael missed Steve Kerr, who was wide open in the corner, and drove to the hoop, only to get clobbered by three defenders. Kerr was the best three-point shooter in the league last year. When Michael went to the free throw line, I asked Steve to inform Michael that he was open, and Steve looked at me and shrugged his shoulders. There was no way he was going to tell the great Michael Jordan how to play the game.

That wasn't surprising. After all, Michael only practiced with the team four times before his first game on March 19, and once he was back in action, his teammates had to compete with the rest of the world for his attention. Everywhere he went, he was surrounded by a squadron of bodyguards and "a personal entourage," who formed a cocoon around him that was difficult to penetrate. In the past Michael sometimes invited friends along on road trips to keep him company and fend off intrusive fans. But now he had the retinue of a small potentate, and when he entered a room, a sea of onlookers gathered around. After a game in Orlando, Toni Kukoc found himself trailing behind the Jordan caravan as it headed from the stadium to the parking lot. Reporters were buzzing around Michael, not even noticing that Toni was there. Parodying Jordan, Kukoc announced to the air, "I'm not giving any interviews."

The first game—at Market Square Arena in Indianapolis— was a three-ring circus, which was broadcast worldwide and attracted the largest TV audience of any regular season NBA game in history. Larry Brown captured the mood perfectly, declaring, "The Beatles and Elvis are back." There were so many cameramen on the floor during warmups, vying for position near Michael, the only thing the other players could do was get out of the way. At one point, observing a TV crew taking footage of Michael's famed Nikes, Corie Blount said, "Now they're interviewing his shoes."

To shake things up, I considered starting Pete Myers at shooting guard instead of Michael, and, in retrospect, I probably should have. Michael's shooting rhythm was off that day: he went 7 for 28 from the field and scored only 19 points in a 103–96 overtime loss. But it wasn't long before he found his stroke. The next weekend he hit a 16-foot jumper to beat Atlanta at the buzzer, then three days later scored 55 points—the highest total in a game to that point in the season—to lead the Bulls past the Knicks at Madison Square Garden. There could be no doubt in anyone's mind that the "real" Michael Jordan was back.

THE SOUL OF TEAMWORK

But there were glitches that bothered me. Many of the players seemed listless and confused when Michael was on the floor. This reminded me of the way the team played when I first joined the Bulls as an assistant coach in 1987. That year Michael had an unprecedented season, winning every honor imaginable, including Most Valuable Player, All-NBA first team, Defensive Player of the Year, All-Star Game MVP, and even Slam Dunk champion, but the members of his "supporting cast," as he called it, were so enthralled by what he could do with a basketball that they never learned to work with him successfully.

After the Knicks game, Michael asked to see me in my office.

"I've decided to quit," he said straightfaced. "What else can I do?"

I made a face.

"No, I'm just kidding," he said, breaking into a smile. But you've got to tell the players they can't expect me to do what I did in New York every night. In our next game I want them to get up and going—to play as a team."

I flashed back to 1989 when I took over as head coach and had talked to Michael about how I wanted him to share the spotlight with his teammates so the team could grow and flourish. In those days he was a gifted young athlete with enormous confidence in his own abilities who had to be cajoled into making sacrifices for the team. Now he was an older, wiser player who understood that it wasn't brilliant individual performances that made great teams, but the energy that's unleashed when players put their egos aside and work toward a common goal.

Good teams become great ones when the members trust each other enough to surrender the "me" for the "we." This is the lesson Michael and his teammates learned en route to winning three consecutive NBA championships. As Bill Cartwright puts it: "A great basketball team will have trust. I've seen teams in this league where the players won't pass to a guy because they don't think he is going to catch the ball. But a great basketball team will throw the ball to everyone. If a guy drops it or bobbles it out of bounds, the next time they'll throw it to him again. And because of their confidence in him, he will have confidence. That's how you grow."

When I was starting out, I, too—like the young, brash Jordan—thought I could conquer the world with the force of my ego, even though my jump shot needed some work. Back then I would have scoffed at anyone who suggested that selflessness and compassion were the secrets to success. Those were qualities that counted in church, not muscling under the boards with Wilt Chamberlain and Kareem Abdul-Jabbar. But after searching long and hard for meaning everywhere else, I discovered that the game itself operated according to laws far more profound than anything that might be found in a coach's playbook. Inside the lines of the court, the mystery of life gets played out night after night.

The first glimpse I had of this came, surprisingly, not on a basketball court, but on a pitcher's mound in Williston, North Dakota.

A JOURNEY OF

A THOUSAND MILES

STARTS WITH

ONE BREATH

For the raindrop, joy is entering the river.
—GHALIB

First I heard a pop, then I felt searing pain in my shoulder, and I knew I was in trouble. Is this it? I said to myself, as I walked off the mound, clutching my arm. Is this the last game I'll ever pitch? I had been virtually untouchable—if a tad wild—that summer pitching for the Williston American Legion team, often fanning 15 or more batters a game with my blinding "80 mph" fastball. Though I had just completed my freshman year at the University of North Dakota on a basketball scholarship, I still harbored fantasies of becoming a major league pitcher. Now I had torn my shoulder, and the future looked bleak.

My brother Joe, who was getting a Ph.D. in psychology at

the University of Texas, suggested self-hypnosis to get my rhythm
back once the injury had healed. The very idea seemed like
blasphemy because of my fundamentalist religious training. I was
wary of giving up control of my mind, even if it was just an
experiment. But my brother, who had been raised in the same
tradition, found a way to break down my resistance. Eventually
my shoulder improved, and the night before my return game, I
agreed to let Joe show me some auto-suggestion techniques,
which, in my case, involved repeating phrases such as "I will be
relaxed" or "I won't throw too hard," to reprogram my subcon-
scious.

The next day I pitched one of my best games ever. Normally
I tried to overpower hitters with my heater, but the more determined I was to blow the ball by a batter, the more reckless I
would become, giving up almost as many walks as strikeouts.
This time, however, I didn't try to force anything—I focused on
the act of throwing the ball and letting the motion flow naturally.
Not only did the nagging pain in my shoulder miraculously disap-
pear, but I also experienced something new for me—near perfect
control. This was my introduction to the hidden power of the
mind and what I could accomplish if I could turn down the
chattering in my head and simply trust my body's innate wisdom.

THE BATTLEGROUND
OF THE MIND

For me, this was a radical idea. It flew in the face of everything
I had been taught as a child about the nature of the mind. I was
trained to keep my mind busy at all times, filling it with passages
from the Bible to prevent evil thoughts from creeping in. When

I was four, my mother hung a large brown paper sign in my bedroom with a quotation from John 3:16: "For God so loved the world, that he gave his only begotten Son, that whosoever believeth in Him should not perish, but have eternal life." From then on I started being concerned with keeping the faith so that I, too, could find eternal life. My mother truly believed that an idle mind was the devil's playground. She gave me hundreds of quotations from the King James Bible to memorize, to keep me armed and ready for the trials and temptations of life. Words and more words—they never stopped.

My mother, Elisabeth, is as passionate about spirituality as anyone I've ever met. She got her calling to become an evangelist when she was a teenager living on a small farm in eastern Montana. One day in the late 1920s, a Pentecostal preacher came to town and won her over. As one of six children from a poor family of German Mennonite homesteaders who had emigrated to Montana from Canada during World War I, she found the idea of being saved by Christ very appealing. After finishing high school, she became a country schoolteacher and then went to Winnipeg Bible College to prepare for her ministry. She traveled all over Montana spreading the Pentecostal message and forming new congregations. She had a voluminous memory and loved to argue theology with anyone foolish enough to take her on. For her, the Bible was a prophetic book, the Word of God, and it predicted that time was running out. The world was headed toward chaos and the Antichrist. It was the midnight hour.

My father, Charles, was a warm, compassionate man with a view of life based on a literal translation of the King James version of the Bible. Once a runaway pickup truck smashed into his car and sent him flying through a window, breaking his arm and putting him in traction for six weeks. The driver of the truck, which was unlicensed, uninsured, and brakeless, was stunned when my father didn't sue. But it didn't surprise any of us. As far as Dad was concerned, litigation was out of the question. It wasn't the Christian thing to do.

Dad was a man of God, pure and simple. He did everything by the Book, and expected me and my brothers, Charles and Joe, to do the same. When we broke one of his many rules, my father would dispense justice swiftly, usually with his razor strap in the cellar of the parsonage. I can remember getting hit only once, and Dad broke into tears while he was doing it. But Joe was not so lucky. He was the rebel in the family. The two of them were always at odds. Once when Joe was ten, he gave my father a Bronx cheer in front of the church after being scolded for some minor indiscretion. Even though he was dressed in a business suit and freshly laundered white shirt, Dad chased Joe down with the rage of Moses, circling the church several times until he caught him. A handful of parishioners looked on, dumbfounded.

My father's first wife died from complications during pregnancy with her second child. Not long afterwards he reconnected with my mother, whom he had met at Bible college, and moved from Ontario with his daughter, Joan, to get married. He was the first member of the Jackson clan to settle in the United States since before the Revolutionary War, when our ancestors, who were English loyalists, had emigrated to Canada. Together, my parents formed a powerful team, working for humble wages at various parishes in Montana and North Dakota. My father was the pastor, making home visitations and delivering sermons on Sundays, while my mother taught Bible classes, played the organ, and gave fire-and-brimstone talks in the evening.

Our lives were dictated by the rhythms of church life. In fact, in my first four years, we actually lived in the basement of the church until the parish could afford a parsonage. Sundays were devoted almost entirely to church activities, and we also had to attend services on Wednesday and Friday evenings. Some weeks we'd spend up to twenty hours in the pews, trying to sit perfectly still under the hawklike gaze of Mom and Dad. The rules in our house were strict. We didn't have a TV, and we were discouraged from going to movies and listening to rock and roll, not to mention experimenting with smoking, drinking, or sex. The point was to be not just an average Christian, but an exceptional one, so when the "end of times" came, we would be chosen. We were taught to believe that the apocalyptic vision in the Book of Revelations was about to be fulfilled any minute, and if we weren't prepared, we'd be left out when Christ returned and gathered up his saints. As a little boy I was terrified of being excluded from the "rapture of saints," as it was called, and losing my parents. One day my mother wasn't home when I returned from school and I got so frightened the rapture had started without me that I ran all over town looking for her. I was shaking when I finally tracked her down at a local radio station, taping a religious program with my dad.

That fear made me a devoted student of the Bible, and my parents had high hopes that I might someday join the ministry. But in my teens, my faith was shaken. The heart of Pentecostal religion is being able to experience the presence of the Holy Spirit physically. This involves "speaking in tongues," a form of ecstatic, highly emotional discourse that sounds like gibberish to the untrained ear. As a boy I had seen thousands "give utterance," as it was called, including my brothers, though I later learned that Joe had doubts about whether his experience was the real thing. But when my turn came, around age twelve or thirteen, *nothing happened.* It was agonizing. I worked hard for the next two or three years, praying long hours, asking forgiveness for my sins and "tarrying for the Spirit" after services. Still nothing. It began to make me skeptical. Why were some people able to do it so easily while others who were far more diligent—namely me—were left speechless? Were all those people making it up? Was it a manufactured experience?

By the time I was fifteen, I realized that, for whatever reason, it wasn't going to happen for me. I began ducking out early at services. My mother didn't hide her disappointment.

"Phil, I noticed you skipped the prayer service," she would say. "You know you've really got to tarry if you want to find the Holy Spirit."

"Well, Mom, I don't know if it's for me."

"Don't say that, Phil. You hurt my spirit when you say things like that. It's for everybody."

What could I do? The act of being filled by the Holy Spirit was *the* central tenet of the Pentecostal faith; it was what separated our sect from other Protestant denominations. I felt like a failure, and yet I couldn't figure out what I was doing wrong. Was it my sinful nature? If so, I didn't feel like a sinner. Was it my lack of faith? Perhaps, but I was no less committed than my brothers. So rather than reject the faith outright, I avoided the issue. I dodged services and started working on my jump shot.

MY SAVIOR: BASKETBALL

Fortunately, I had an outlet for my energy in which success came easily—basketball. I was 6'6" in high school—and would grow to 6'8" in college—with square shoulders and arms so long I could sit in the back seat of a car and open both front doors at the same time. My classmates poked fun at my gangling physique and nicknamed me "Bones," but I didn't mind because I loved the game. In 1963, my senior year, I led Williston High to the state championship, scoring 48 points in the tournament final. The next thing I knew, I was being hotly pursued by the new coach at the University of North Dakota, Bill Fitch.

One reason for my early success was my fierce competitive drive, honed over the years by battling two older brothers at everything from checkers to one-on-one hoops. Charles and Joe, six and four years older, respectively, made fun of me when I tried to compete with them, and their laughter drove me to try even harder. No doubt I inherited some of that spirit from my mother, who was a basketball player in high school and turned every activity—ironing shirts, playing Scrabble, hiking with her Sunday school class—into an Olympic sport. For me, winning was a matter of life and death. As a kid, I often threw temper tantrums when I lost, especially if I was competing against my brothers. Losing made me feel humiliated and worthless, as if I didn't exist. Once during a high school baseball tournament, I was called in as a reliever and pitched nearly perfect ball for several innings. But I was inconsolable when we lost, even though it was probably my best performance that year. I just sat in the dugout after the game and wept.

My obsession with winning was often my undoing. I would push so hard to succeed when things weren't going my way that it would hurt my performance. That's the lesson I learned after my self-hypnosis session with Joe. I was trying to force my body to cooperate, and, when it didn't respond, my mind became even more insistent. But on the pitcher's mound that day I discovered that I could be effective, even overcome pain, by letting go and *not* thinking. It was an important turning point for me. Though

I soon gave up baseball to pursue a basketball career, the feeling of freedom I experienced during that game stayed with me and made me curious about finding a way to re-create it consistently.

That weekend Joe also introduced me to Zen Buddhism, which he had been experiencing with one of his professors at the University of Texas. His description of Zen baffled me. How could you have a religion that didn't involve belief in God—or at least the personalized idea of God I was familiar with? What did Zen practitioners do? Joe said they simply tried to clear their minds and be in the present. To someone raised in a Pentecostal household—where attention was focused more on the hereafter than the here and now—this was a mind-boggling concept.

Inspired by those discussions, I signed up for a combined major of psychology, philosophy, and religion when I returned for my sophomore year at UND and began to expand my intellectual horizons. Sensing, no doubt, that I could use some worldly wisdom, coach Bill Fitch had me room with Paul Pederson, one of the stars of the team. Pederson had been raised as a Lutheran and had a healthy skepticism about institutionalized religion. He encouraged me to take a detached look at the belief system I had been spoon-fed since childhood and explore life more freely. It was a heady feeling. The sixties were in full swing, and I immersed myself in the counterculture—or at least the version that had made its way to North Dakota. I hung out with some rather dissident friends on campus and started catching up on rock and roll, Fellini movies, and other fine points of contemporary life that I'd missed out on in high school. I also began dating my first wife, Maxine, a political science major and student leader who inspired me to become more active politically. In 1967, my senior year, we got married, and had a daughter, Elizabeth.

What appealed to me about the sixties—and what I carried

away with me when it was over—was the emphasis on compassion and brotherhood, getting together and loving one another *right now*, to paraphrase The Youngbloods. Many people were on the same path, trying to escape from their parents' archaic views and reinvent the world. I no longer felt so isolated from my peers. For the first time in my life, I wasn't an outsider looking in.

My basketball career took off, too. Fitch, who later became an NBA coach, was a stern taskmaster who taught me discipline and how to play without fear. I wasn't exactly a selfless player: I had a tendency to try and score every time I got the ball, without even looking to see if one of my teammates had a better shot. But that didn't worry Fitch as long as I played selflessly when it really counted: executing his trademark full-court defense. In my junior year I averaged 21.8 points and, to my surprise, was named a first-team All-American, along with future teammates Walt Frazier and Earl Monroe. That year North Dakota, which had a lackluster record before Fitch arrived, made it to the NCAA (college division) finals for the second year in a row, and the NBA scouts began to notice me. One of them was my future boss, Jerry Krause, then a scout for the Baltimore Bullets, who wrote that he liked my hook shot and my "better than average moves inside." New York's Red Holzman also gave me a favorable report, and, after I made the All-American team again as a senior, the Knicks drafted me in the second round.

THE HOLZMAN SCHOOL OF MANAGEMENT

On my first visit to New York, Holzman and his wife, Selma, picked me up the airport. As we were driving along the expressway into Manhattan, a teenager threw a rock at the car from an overpass and smashed the windshield. Red was furious. I expected him to turn around and chase after the kid. But when he realized that nobody was hurt, he lightened up. "Well, that's New York City, Phil," he said, brushing off the incident. "If you can take that, you'll do just fine here."

Thus began my course in the Holzman school of management.

Lesson one: Don't let anger—or heavy objects thrown from overpasses—cloud the mind.

Holzman was no Eastern philosopher, but he understood instinctively the importance of awareness in building championship teams. Playing under him, I transformed from a me-first hotshot into a multidimensional team player with a deeper understanding of the inner game of basketball. The lessons I learned from Red provided the foundation for the selfless approach to teamwork that I would later develop with the Bulls.

Red took over as coach of the Knicks in the middle of my rookie year, and it was clear from the first practice what he was looking for. He wanted us to be in tune with each other and what was happening on court at all times. That was true even if you were riding the bench. Once during a timeout at the end of a game, I was goofing around on the sidelines with backup center Nate Bowman when Red suddenly stormed down the floor, stuck his nose in my face and asked, "How much time is left, Jackson?"

"A minute and twenty-eight seconds," I said.

"No. How much time is left on the twenty-four-second clock?"

"Uh, I don't know."

"Well, you've got to know, because you may be going into the game, and if you don't know the time, you could get us in trouble. Don't let me catch you doing that again."

He didn't.

Lesson two: Awareness is everything.

Holzman was a master of defense. In fact, during that first practice, he had us running up and down the floor, applying full-court pressure. Red believed that hard-nosed defense not only won big games, but also, and more importantly, forced players to develop solidarity as a team. On offense a great scorer can often dominate a game, and players frequently place their own individual goals of pumping up their scoring average ahead of what's best for the team. But on defense everybody has the same mission—stopping the enemy—and you can't get far trying to do it single-handedly.

The Knicks were so loaded with good shooters—Walt Frazier, Bill Bradley, Cazzie Russell—Holzman didn't concern himself about offense. He let us design our own plays. We had the D play for Dave DeBusschere to set him up for an easy outside shot. And for Bradley, we ran the Princeton Tiger play, which he had used in college when he was being double- and triple-teamed. What was important to Holzman was that we keep the ball moving and not let one or two players get all the shots. As a result, we often had six to eight players in double figures.

Lesson three: The power of We is stronger than the power of Me.

To survive on the Knicks, I had to carve out a new role for myself. Coming off the bench I couldn't be "The Man" anymore, so I focused on improving my defense. Luckily, Holzman's high-pressure style of defense came easily to me because it resembled Bill Fitch's. That year, on the strength of my defensive play, I was selected to the All-Rookie team and started fantasizing about breaking into the starting lineup.

Then disaster struck.

Midway through my second year, I went up for a turnaround jump shot in Oakland, got bumped by Clyde Lee, and came down hard on my heels, herniating two disks in my vertebrae. The injury required spinal-fusion surgery and sidelined me for that season and the next. I had to spend the first six months in a back brace. The pain was excruciating—and many of my standard options for distracting myself were off limits. Basketball was out. Sex was out. Overnight, Action Jackson had become Traction Jackson.

To entertain myself, I began observing my thoughts and trying to figure out what made my mind click. What I discovered was a mountain of guilt. I felt guilty about my back injury, which could have easily ended my career. I felt guilty about my marriage, which had been showing signs of strain ever since Maxine and I had moved to New York. I felt guilty about not spending enough time with my daughter. Though I still occasionally went to church, I felt guilty about distancing myself from my parents and my spiritual heritage. Why did I put so much pressure on myself? Would I ever be able to escape all those years of Bible school conditioning?

Obviously, I wasn't as liberated as I thought.

When my injury healed, the Knicks decided to keep me off the roster for the 1969–70 season to protect me from the expansion draft. During that period Holzman adopted me as his assistant coach *ex officio*. I practiced with the team, scouted upcoming opponents, and discussed strategy with Red before and after games. I learned how to look at the game from the perspective of what the *whole* team was doing and to conceptualize ways to disrupt an opponent's game plan. In short, I began to think like a coach.

The nucleus of the Knicks' championship team was already formed. Shortly after I was injured, forward Cazzie Russell broke his leg, which cut the roster down to nine players, three of whom were rookies. That meant that the starting five—guards Walt Frazier and Dick Barnett, center Willis Reed, and forwards Bill Bradley and Dave DeBusschere—had to average forty minutes or more per game—at an all-out Holzmanesque pace. To survive, they had to forge themselves into a harmonious working unit. All they needed was a stronger bench, which happened in 1969–70, when Russell and forward Dave Stallworth returned to the lineup. The team took off early that season and persevered to win the championship.

THE GIFT OF AWARENESS

When I came back the next year, I knew I would no longer be able to rely solely on talent to carry me through. I would have to use my mind more effectively to offset my loss of flexibility and quickness. Ultimately the key would be to increase my level of awareness. My teacher was Bill Bradley. Unlike DeBusschere, who liked to take it easy in practice, Bradley demanded constant attention. He wasn't that fast, but he had an uncanny sense of court awareness. If your mind wandered for a millisecond, he'd vanish into thin air, then reappear on the other side of the court with a wide open shot.

Covering him in practice showed me just how weak my

powers of concentration were. I had been a center in college and, by instinct, focused on following the ball and protecting the basket. But Bradley was such a great player off the ball, I had to learn how to attach myself to him without being distracted and losing track of what was happening on the rest of the floor. To train myself to be relaxed and fully alert, I began practicing visualization. I would sit quietly for fifteen or twenty minutes before the game in a secluded part of the stadium—my favorite place was the New York Rangers' locker room—and create a moving picture in my mind of what was about to happen. I'd call up images of the man I was going to cover and visualize myself stopping his moves. That was the first part. The next step, which was much harder, was to lay back and not try to force the action once the game started, but to allow it to unfold *naturally*. Playing basketball isn't a linear thought process: "Okay, when Joe Blow takes that funny drop step over there I'm going to jump in and do my Bill Russell imitation." The idea was to code the image of a successful move into my visual memory so that when a similar situation emerged in a game it would seem, to paraphrase Yogi Berra, like déjà vu all over again.

A turning point came in the fifth game of the 1971–72 playoffs in Boston. Bradley had been having trouble guarding the Celtics' crafty Don Nelson, so Holzman put me on him. One of Nelson's tricks was to load up his fingers with pine tar resin so that the ball would stick to his fingers when he faked a shot. This was maddening for me because I had a quick trigger in blocking shots. To beat him, I had to pick the move apart in my head, step by step, then try to remain clearheaded so that when he finally made his move I would recognize the moment and do what I had to do. It worked. The first time Nelson tried to fake me out in that game, I didn't get tense and overreact because I knew what was going to happen. That clarity allowed me to stick with him and throw him off his game, creating some important scoring opportunities for us that helped seal the victory.

We beat Boston in that series, 4–1, but without Willis Reed, who was recovering from knee surgery, we weren't able to get past Wilt Chamberlain and the Lakers in the finals. All that changed the following year when Reed returned, and the addition of center-forward Jerry Lucas and guards Earl Monroe and Dean Meminger gave us the most versatile attack in the NBA. The critical point in the playoffs came in the seventh game of the Eastern Conference finals, against the Celtics again in Boston Garden. During a film session the night before, Holzman pointed out that the Celtics were disrupting our full-court press by having their forwards set picks upcourt against the slight 6'1" Meminger.

"You've got to get through those picks, Dean," said Red.

"I can't—they're too big," replied Meminger.

" 'I can't' is no excuse. Get through the picks!"

The next day Meminger was relentless, breaking picks, containing Jo-Jo White, and scoring 26 points as we abolished the myth of the Celtics' invulnerability in the Garden. Before that day, they'd never lost a seventh playoff game on their home floor.

After that series, the finals against L.A. seemed anticlimactic. Chamberlain was ineffective, and we flew past the Lakers in five games to clinch the title. The postgame festivities in L.A. were exhilarating. This was the pinnacle of my sports career to that point, the moment I had been striving for with all my heart since I was a kid. And yet two days later when we gathered again in New York for a celebration with family and friends at Tavern on the Green, suddenly the thrill was gone. The room was crowded with celebrities—Robert Redford held court in one corner, Dustin Hoffman in another—but the intense feeling of connection with my teammates I had experienced in L.A. seemed like a distant memory. Instead of being overwhelmed with joy, I felt empty and confused. Was this *it*? I kept saying to myself. Is *this* what was supposed to bring me happiness?

Clearly the answer lay somewhere else.

chapter THREE

IF YOU MEET THE BUDDHA

IN THE LANE, FEED HIM

THE BALL

*Our own life is the instrument with which
we experiment with the truth.*
—THICH NHAT HANH

What I was missing was spiritual direction. The unfulfilled legacy of my devout childhood had left an emptiness, a yearning to reconnect with the deeper mysteries of life.

In 1972 my marriage fell apart. Maxine felt isolated and unfulfilled living in Queens and being an NBA "widow," and I wasn't ready to commit myself to family life. We parted amicably, and I moved into a loft above an auto repair shop in the Chelsea district of Manhattan.

The man I purchased the apartment from was a lapsed Catholic turned fundamentalist Muslim named Hakim. We soon became friends, and every week or so we would have dinner at the loft and check up on each other's spiritual progress. Hakim, a graduate student in psychology who had grown up in an Italian neighborhood in Brooklyn, was drawn to the Muslim faith because he had lived on the edge for years and felt he needed a strict canon of rules to put his life back in order. I was looking for just the opposite: a way to express myself spiritually without giving up my newfound freedom.

One evening, during a moment of quiet reflection, Hakim told me he had a vision of my childhood. "I see you as a little boy sitting in a high chair," he said. "You want to eat with your left hand, but your mother is forcing you to use your right. She's hovering over you, shoving the spoon into your right hand and making sure you use it. Meanwhile, your father's in the background, smiling and allowing it to happen."

Hakim had never met my parents, but he understood the dynamic in my family with uncanny accuracy. When I was little, my mother tried to force me to submit to her will, cramming my head with Bible passages, making me eat with my right hand instead of my left, while my father looked on benignly and loved me unconditionally, no matter what I did. It struck me listening to Hakim that I had inherited my mother's mind and my father's heart, and those two sides of my character were still in conflict. The part of me that was like my mother, always searching for logical answers, always trying to exert control, usually won out over the part that, like my father, was moved by compassion, trusting the song in my heart.

One summer in Montana around this time, my parents, Joe, and I got into a heated theological debate after dinner—a common occurrence whenever you got two or more Jacksons in a room. Early in the evening, my father checked out and went to bed. When I asked him the next day why he had left the conversation, he replied, "Arguing isn't where faith is. That just feeds the ego. It's all in the doing." To him, there were certain mysteries that you could only understand with the heart, and intellectualizing about them was a waste of time. He accepted God on faith and lived his life accordingly. This was an important lesson for me.

There's a passage in Carlos Castaneda's *The Teachings of Don Juan*, in which Don Juan advises Castaneda: "Look at every path closely and deliberately. Try it as many times as you think necessary. Then ask yourself, and yourself alone the question. . . . Does this path have a heart? If it does, the path is good. If it doesn't, it is of no use."

That was the question I had to ask myself.

I started exploring a variety of paths. Inspired by *Sunseed*, a film about the search for enlightenment, I began taking yoga classes, reading books about Eastern religion, and attending lectures by Krishnamurti, Pir Vilayat Khan, and other spiritual teachers. By then my brother Joe had left academia and moved to the Lama Foundation in New Mexico to experience the Sufi way. I visited him there and participated in many of the rituals. Much to my surprise, the more I studied other traditions, the more intrigued I became about taking another look at my spiritual roots.

REAWAKENING

At the time Christianity was going through its "Godspell" phase. The charismatic movement, a kinder, gentler version of Pentecostalism, was in full swing, and everyone from Methodists to Unitarians and Roman Catholics had woven elements of sixties culture into their services. That made it easier for me to poke my head back in the door.

What interested me most was revelation, though not in the way I remembered it from childhood: scenes of men and women so overcome by divine bliss their bodies quivered and their mouths went on automatic. Frankly, the idea of being swept away in a paroxysm of emotion, no matter what the benefits, made *me* quiver. Perhaps there was a less histrionic way to experience the Holy Spirit.

On one of the Knicks' road trips, I picked up a copy of William James' *The Varieties of Religious Experience*, a book filled with firsthand accounts by Quakers, Shakers, and other Christian mystics. I couldn't put it down. Reading their stories, it was clear that mystical experience didn't have to be a big production. It didn't require hallucinogenic drugs or a major Pentecostal-style catharsis. It could be as uneventful as a moment of reflection.

When I finished the book, I put it down, said a prayer and, all of a sudden, experienced a quiet feeling of inner peace. Nothing special—and yet there it was. This was the experience I had longed for as a teenager. It wasn't the big, crashing moment of transcendence that I expected, but it came close enough to give me an idea of what I had been missing. It also gave me a deeper understanding of my Pentecostal roots and helped lift the curtain of guilt that had shrouded me most of my life. I no longer felt compelled to run from my past or cling to it out of fear. I could take from it what worked for me and let the rest go. I could also explore other traditions more fully without feeling as if I was committing a major sacrilege against God and family.

ZEN BONES

My next step was to explore meditation. First I tried the simple breath-counting technique outlined in Lawrence LeShan's book, *How to Meditate*. That kept me busy for a while, but it was devoid of spiritual content and began to feel like mental calisthenics. I turned to Joel Goldsmith's *Practicing the Presence*, a book that attempts to bridge the gap between East and West by using Christian maxims as guidelines for meditation. Goldsmith demythologized meditation and helped me understand it within a Christian context. But the technique he recommended, which involved visualization and repeating inspirational phrases, was far too cerebral for me. The last thing I needed was to increase my level of mental activity.

Then I turned to Zen. Though my brother Joe had already introduced me to the basics, it wasn't until the mid-seventies that I started practicing seriously, using *Zen Mind, Beginner's Mind*, by the late Japanese roshi, Shunryu Suzuki, as my guide. One summer I began sitting with a small group of Zen students in Montana who were connected with the Mt. Shasta Abbey in northern California. By then I had remarried, to my present wife, June, and had another daughter, Chelsea. When I met June a few years earlier at a pinochle game in New York, she had just graduated from the University of Connecticut and was working at a job she hated at Bellevue Hospital. I invited her to spend the summer traveling around the northwest on my motorcycle. After that magical trip, June moved into my loft, and marriage soon followed.

The summer I discovered the Mt. Shasta group, Joe and I were consumed with building a vacation home for my family on

Flathead Lake. Every morning at 5:30 he and I would start the day with a half hour of meditation, then in the afternoon we'd take a break to do Sufi grounding exercises. After we finished putting up the rough-cut pole-and-beam frame, we recruited one of the members of the Zen group to help us build the deck. I was impressed by his demeanor as he worked. He was fast and efficient, and radiated a peaceful self-assurance, developed through years of daily Zen practice, that put everyone at ease.

What appealed to me about Zen was its emphasis on clearing the mind. As the Buddha put it in the Dhammapada, "Everything is based on mind, is led by mind, is fashioned by mind. If you speak and act with a polluted mind, suffering will follow you, as the wheels of an oxcart follow the footsteps of the ox. . . . If you speak and act with a pure mind, happiness will follow you, as a shadow clings to a form." But the Zen idea of a polluted mind is quite different from the traditional Christian perspective, which dictates that "impure" thoughts be rooted out and eliminated. What pollutes the mind in the Buddhist view is our desire to get life to conform to our peculiar notion of how things *should* be, as opposed to how they really are. In the course of everyday life, we spend the majority of our time immersed in self-centered thoughts. *Why did this happen to me? What would make* me *feel better? If only I could make more money, win her heart, make my boss appreciate me.* The thoughts themselves are not the problem; it's our desperate clinging to them and our resistance to what's actually happening that causes us so much anguish.

There's an old Zen story that illustrates this point. Two monks were traveling together in a heavy downpour when they came upon a beautiful woman in a silk kimono who was having trouble crossing a muddy intersection. "Come on," said the first monk to the woman, and he carried her in his arms to a dry spot. The second monk didn't say anything until much later. Then he couldn't contain himself anymore. "We monks don't go near females," he said. "Why did you do that?"

"I left the woman back there," the first monk replied. "Are you still carrying her?"

The point of Zen practice is to make you aware of the thoughts that run your life and diminish their power over you. One of the fundamental tools for doing that is a form of sitting meditation known as *zazen*. The form of zazen I practice involves sitting completely still on a cushion with the eyes open but directed downward and focusing attention on the breath. When thoughts come up, the idea is not to try to blot them out or to analyze them, but simply to note them as they arise, and to experience, as fully as possible, the sensations in the body. When you do that regularly, day after day, you begin to see how ephemeral your thoughts are and become acutely aware of your bodily sensations and what's going on around you—the sound of the traffic in the distance, the smell of the flowers across the room. Over time your thoughts calm down, first for a few seconds, then much longer, and you experience moments of *just being* without your mind getting in the way.

I found the Zen perspective on concentration particularly intriguing. According to Suzuki, concentration comes not from trying hard to focus on something, but from keeping your mind open and directing it at nothing. "Concentration means freedom," he writes in *Zen Mind, Beginner's Mind*. "In zazen practice we say your mind should be concentrated on your breathing, but the way to keep your mind on your breathing is to forget all about yourself and just to sit and feel your breathing. If you are concentrated on your breathing, you will forget yourself, and if you forget yourself you will be concentrated on your breathing."

As a basketball player, this made a lot of sense to me. I knew from experience that I was far more effective when my mind was clear and I wasn't playing with an agenda of some kind, like scoring a certain number of points or showing up one of my opponents. The more skilled I became at watching my thoughts in zazen practice, the more focused I became as a player. I also developed an intimate knowledge of my mental processes on the basketball court.

My thoughts took many forms. There was pure self-interest ("When I get the ball, I'm going for the hoop, no matter what") and selfless self-interest ("When I get the ball, I'm going to pass it to Bradley, no matter what"). There was anger ("That #$%^&* Wilt Chamberlain. Next time he's dead meat") and fear ("That #$%^&* Chamberlain. Next time I'll let Willis handle him"). There was self-praise ("That was cool. Do it again") and, more likely in my case, self-blame ("What's wrong with you, Phil? A sixth grader could make that shot"). The litany was endless. However, the simple act of becoming mindful of the frenzied parade of thoughts, paradoxically, began to quiet my mind down.

Basketball happens at such a fast pace that your mind has a tendency to race at the same speed as your pounding heart. As the pressure builds, it's easy to start thinking too much. But if you're always trying to figure the game out, you won't be able to respond creatively to what's going on. Yogi Berra once said about baseball: "How can you think and hit at the same time?" The same is true with basketball, except everything's happening much faster. The key is seeing and doing. If you're focusing on anything other than reading the court and doing what needs to be done, the moment will pass you by.

Sitting zazen, I learned to *trust the moment*—to immerse myself in action as mindfully as possible, so that I could react spontaneously to whatever was taking place. When I played without "putting a head on top of a head," as one Zen teacher puts it, I found that my true nature as an athlete emerged. It's not uncommon for basketball players, especially young ones, to expend a great deal of mental energy trying to be somebody they're not. But once you get caught up in that game, it's a losing battle. I discovered that I was far more effective when I became completely immersed in the action, rather than trying to control it and fill my mind with unrealistic expectations.

WHERE THE RIVERS MEET

Another aspect of Zen that intrigued me was its emphasis on compassion. The goal of Zen is not just to clear the mind, but to open the heart as well. The two, of course, are interrelated. Awareness is the seed of compassion. As we begin to notice ourselves and others, just as we are, without judgment, compassion flows naturally.

Compassion is where Zen and Christianity intersect. Though I still have reservations about the more rigid aspects of Christianity, I have always been deeply moved by the fundamental insight that love is a conquering force. In I Corinthians 13:1–2, St. Paul writes: "If I speak in the tongues of men and angels but do not have love, I am a noisy gong or a clanging cymbal. And if I have prophetic power, and understand all mysteries and knowledge, and I have all faith, so as to remove mountains, but do not have love, I am nothing."

When I was a boy, I was so caught up in the mental aspects of worship—building a wall in my mind with prayers and quotations from the Bible—that I lost track of the essence of Christianity. But by practicing Zen, I was able to clear my mind of all that interference and open my heart again. Merging Zen and Christianity allowed me to reconnect with my spiritual core and begin to integrate my heart and mind. The more I learned about the similarities between the two religions, the more compatible they seemed. Was Christ a Zen master? That may be a stretch, but clearly he was practicing some form of meditation when he separated himself from his disciples and became one with "the Father."

What does all this have to do with professional basketball? Compassion is not exactly the first quality one looks for in a player. But as my practice matured, I began to appreciate the importance of playing with an open heart. Love is the force that ignites the spirit and binds teams together.

Obviously, there's an intellectual component to playing basketball. Strategy is important. But once you've done the mental work, there comes a point when you have to throw yourself into the action and put your heart on the line. That means not only being brave, but also being compassionate, toward yourself, your teammates, and your opponents. This idea was an important building block of my philosophy as a coach. More than anything else, what allowed the Bulls to sustain a high level of excellence was the players' compassion for each other.

Pro basketball is a macho sport. Many coaches, worried about showing any sign of weakness, tend to shut down emotionally and ostracize players who aren't meeting their expectations. This can have a disturbing ripple effect on the players that undermines team unity. Late in my career the Knicks acquired Spencer Haywood, one of the game's premier forwards, to strengthen the front line. When he arrived, he announced to the press that he was going to be "the next Dave DeBusschere" and was so cocky everybody on the team, not to mention the fans, started secretly waiting for him to fail. Haywood lived up to his own hype at first—much to my dismay, since he had replaced me as a starter—but a year or two later he began to have trouble leaping. Initially the doctors were baffled by his condition, so the coaching staff, and then the players, became convinced that he was faking it. Everybody treated him as if he were a leper, and his performance deteriorated even further. It wasn't until the off-season that the doctors learned that Haywood had a nerve problem in his leg that could be partially remedied by surgery. But by then the damage to the team had already been done.

In my work as a coach, I've discovered that approaching problems of this kind from a compassionate perspective, trying to empathize with the player and look at the situation from his point of view, can have a transformative effect on the team. Not only does it reduce the player's anxiety and make him feel as if someone understands what he's going through, it also inspires the other players to respond in kind and be more conscious of each other's needs.

The most dramatic example of this occurred in 1990 when Scottie Pippen's father died while we were in the middle of a tough playoff series against the Philadelphia 76ers. Pippen skipped Game 4 to attend the funeral and was still in a solemn mood before the start of the next game. I thought it was important for the team to acknowledge what was going on with Scottie and give him support. I asked the players to form a circle around him in the locker room and recite the Lord's Prayer, as we often do on Sundays. "We may not be Scottie's family," I said, "but we're as close to him as anyone in his life. This is a critical time for him. We should tell him how much we love him and show compassion for his loss." Demonstrations of heartfelt affection are rare in the NBA, and Scottie was visibly moved. That night, buoyed by his teammates, he went on a 29-point romp, as we finished off the 76ers to take the series.

In the next series, against the Pistons, the stress finally took its toll on Scottie, and just before the seventh game he came down with a migraine headache that gave him double vision. Some members of the press speculated that Scottie, who didn't have a history of migraines, must be faking it and blamed him for the team's heartbreaking defeat. I was as disappointed by the loss as anyone, but I defended Scottie because I knew that his suffering was real. The players were deeply affected by my compassion for Scottie, and rallied behind him. That spirit was the seed from which a championship team would grow.

CHANGE: THE UNINVITED GUEST

I can empathize with players because I, too, have been through painful experiences in this game. The most humbling was when my playing career ended. To me, this was a kind of death. It meant giving up my identity as as warrior, my *raison d'etre* since boyhood, and becoming, in my view, a nonperson. I wasn't prepared psychologically when it finally happened.

In 1978 I was traded to the New Jersey Nets. Toward the end of training camp that year, the Nets' coach, Kevin Loughery, asked me to go for a ride with him in his car. I was thirty-three at the time, and the Nets were loaded with young, talented players. I figured Loughery was going to cut me, but he threw me a curve. "Basically, Phil, we're in a difficult situation," he said. "You've had a good run and I hate to tell anyone he's through playing ball. But I'd like you to stay here as an assistant coach. We've got a lot of young kids who don't know how to play yet. I'd like you to dress for practices and play against them, just in case we need you for a game, but mostly I want you to be a coach."

Me? A coach? Just four years earlier I had written in my autobiography, *Maverick*, that I could never imagine myself coaching in the NBA. Now here it was—a reality. Coaching seemed like an impossible profession: watching, critiquing, dealing with egocentric players like me. I had coached Pee Wee and Babe Ruth League baseball teams in college, and enjoyed teaching fundamentals and plotting strategy. But baseball is a simple, linear game, while basketball is a complex, ever-changing flow, all happening under the intense glare of the TV cameras. Was I ready for this?

Loughery didn't have any doubts. His confidence in me helped me make the transition to coaching, which turned out to be more gradual than I expected. (Over the next two years, he often inserted me in the lineup to fill in for injured players.) Loughery had a subtle intuitive gift, and often surprised me with his insights about the team. During the 1978–79 season the Nets got off to the best start in the history of the franchise, but Loughery was skeptical. He felt that early success had spoiled the players, and nobody was listening to him anymore. One night after a home game, he told the general manager, Charlie Theokas, he wanted to quit. An emergency meeting of the coaches and management followed in the equipment room.

"Kevin, how could you possibly think about leaving this

team?" implored owner Joe Taub. "We're ten games over .500. This is the best we've ever played, and we're not even halfway through the season. Who's going to replace you?"

Loughery looked around the room.

"Phil. He can coach the team."

"He doesn't have enough experience."

"Sure, he does."

My heart went into overdrive. When Taub turned to me, I said, "Yeah, I can coach this team," and, in my naiveté, I actually thought I could. But it would have been a disaster. Loughery was right: the Nets were a flashy, fast-starting team that didn't have the courage or desire to go all the way. They would fade early that year, just barely making the playoffs with a 37–45 record.

Management persuaded Loughery to stay and he let me step in for him every now and then when he was tossed out of games. One night I took over in a close game on the road against the Seattle Supersonics. We went ahead down the stretch, but with six seconds left, Seattle's Gus Williams tied the score. I called a timeout to set up the final play. As the players came off the floor, John Lee Williamson, a cocksure shooting guard who loved to take pressure shots, said to me, "You're going to go with 'The Man,' aren't you?"

"The Man" he was referring to, of course, was himself.

"No," I replied, put off by his arrogance. "I'm going to go with Eric Money."

Money was having a good game, and I thought we could surprise the Sonics by having him take the shot. But he didn't live up to his name. As he started his move to the basket, Gus Williams stole the ball from him and drove the length of the court for the game-winning layup. After the game, Williamson came striding over to me in the locker room and said, "I guess that'll teach you a lesson—you go with 'The Man' down the stretch." I hated to admit it, but he was right. I realized that I had been reacting to his arrogant manner rather than doing what was best for the team.

DEATH AND REBIRTH

That wasn't the only lesson I had to learn. In fact, it would take years—and coaching jobs in Albany and Puerto Rico—before I'd master the subtleties of the game well enough to coach in the NBA. But first I had to step away from basketball and put my life as a player behind me. I also had one more lesson to learn from my father.

In June 1979 Dad was diagnosed with cancer and had part of one of his lungs removed. He was seventy-three years old at the time and calmly reminded us after the operation that, according to the Bible, a man is given three score and ten years. A few days later the doctors told my brother Joe and I that he was in good enough shape to return home. "Well, you're getting out of here tomorrow, Dad," I said, trying to sound upbeat.

"I don't know," he replied. "I want you guys to pray for me to go home."

"What do you mean? You're going home tomorrow."

"No, I don't mean *that* home."

Joe and I looked at each other, knowingly. The next morning we learned that he had died of a heart attack during the night.

My brothers and I and Hal Rylands, a close family friend, dug my father's grave at the Big Fork, Montana, cemetery. While we were working, an English sparrow appeared out of nowhere and started fluttering around the gravesite. Suddenly it became clear that this was no ordinary bird. It seemed to have no fear at all. It flew up to me and alighted on my shoulder. Then it darted around and touched everyone in the group. My Lakota Sioux friends would say that the bird was my father's spirit bidding us farewell.

Though I sorely missed him, my father's death had a liberating effect on me. As long as he was alive, I felt a certain pressure to keep up appearances. He was a respected minister, and I didn't want to embarrass him by not going to services, particularly during the off-season when I spent a lot of time in Montana. It wasn't until he died that I felt that I could finally break from my past without guilt and become more fully myself.

EXPERIMENTS

IN THE COCKROACH

BASKETBALL LEAGUE

It is good to have an end to journey toward;
but it is the journey that matters, in the end.
—URSULA K. LeGUIN

To this point, my spiritual journey had been primarily a private affair. I rarely talked about it with my teammates, and didn't fully understand how to apply the wisdom I had learned on the meditation cushion to the competitive world of professional basketball. It wasn't until I became coach of my own team that I began to see for the first time how to make that leap.

After spending an unfulfilling year in Montana running a health club and trying to get a junior college basketball program off the ground, I was offered a job in 1982 coaching the Albany Patroons in the Continental Basketball League. It wasn't exactly a dream situation: the team was 8–17 when I arrived, and the players had been in open revolt against the coach, my ex-Knick teammate Dean Meminger. Turning the Patroons around was going to take a major dose of creativity.

One advantage of working in Albany was that I could move my family, which now included four children—Chelsea, Brooke, and the twins, Charley and Ben—to Woodstock. It wasn't Montana, but it was far enough from New York City so that I could remain anonymous. The free-flowing intellectual atmosphere in Woodstock also inspired me to be more inventive as a coach. In the world of professional basketball, Albany was about as far away from the big time as you could get. It was a good place to experiment with unorthodox concepts.

My accomplice was Charley Rosen, a novelist/basketball aficionado (and the co-author of *Maverick*) who became attached to the Patroons after helping me out with training camp. The CBA didn't allow teams to have assistant coaches then, so Charley, who had studied physiology in college, volunteered to be the trainer. He was paid only $25 a game and had to wear a white uniform on court that made him look like a Good Humor man. But he didn't care because he loved the game. He especially enjoyed batting ideas around with me about how to revolutionize basketball.

Rosen and I were a good match. He saw everything in black and white; I saw infinite gradations of gray. He was obsessed with pinpointing the exact moment when everything turned to dung and who was to blame—more often than not, a referee. I was more interested in the quality of the team's energy as it ebbed and flowed, and figuring out what lessons could be learned when disaster struck. As my wife likes to say, I can "smell a rose in a pile of manure."

SEEDING THE GROUP MIND

Although I had worked briefly as an assistant coach in the NBA, I didn't have any formal training. But I did have a grand scheme: I wanted to create a team in which selflessness—not the me-first mentality that had come to dominate professional basketball— was the primary driving force. My goal was to find a structure that would empower *everybody* on the team, not just the stars, and allow the players to grow as individuals as they surrendered themselves to the group effort.To mold the Patroons into a "selfless" team, I arranged for everybody to receive the same salary, $330 a week, and distributed playing time more democratically. We had ten players on the roster, so I divided them into two five-man units—the first and second teams—and rotated them into the game *as units* in eight-minute intervals. For the last eight minutes, I'd use a unit made up of the players who had the hottest hands that day.

Giving everybody playing time helped defuse a lot of the petty jealousy that usually fragments teams. It worked so well, in fact, that it became one of my trademarks as a coach. Casey Stengel, the famed skipper of the New York Yankees, once said that the key to coaching was to keep the five or six guys who got little or no playing time from banding together and poisoning the minds of everyone else on the team. I take a somewhat different tack. While most NBA coaches use only seven or eight players regularly, particularly during the playoffs, I try to work all twelve players on the roster into the rotation, to keep everybody's mind focused on the same goal. The players were skeptical, at first, but toward the end of my inaugural season, they got a taste of what could happen if they really supported each other: they beat the CBA All-Stars in an exhibition game. After that, they started paying closer attention when I talked about selfless team play.

One thing I learned in the CBA was how important it is to inspire players to commit to the team effort even though everything else was pushing them in another direction. The CBA was a showcase league. Most of the players were in their early twenties and, for various reasons, had missed out on making the NBA. Their dream was to be spotted by one of the scouts that toured the league and get another shot at the big money. It happened all the time, and often had a disruptive effect on the team. Just as we'd take off on a winning streak, the NBA would swoop in and pick off our best players, and the minds of those who stayed behind went with them.

So I constantly had to figure out ways to get the players to strengthen their commitment. When Vince Lombardi was a basketball coach at Fordham in the early 1940s, he used to have his players make a pledge before each practice. He'd stand them behind the end line and say "God has ordained me to teach you young men about basketball today. I want all those who want that training to step across that line." This wasn't just an empty symbolic gesture. Lombardi understood the power of making a conscious act of commitment. That's why he wanted his players to cross that line every day.

The CBA was not as homogenized as a Catholic men's college. The players were from all kinds of backgrounds, and many had never even finished high school. If I tried to pull a Lombardi, they would have looked at me as though I was a visitor from another planet. As I got to know them better, however, I found that most of them resonated with the idea of surrendering to something larger than themselves. Though their behavior on court often indicated otherwise, most of them secretly yearned to connect with the group and were willing to sacrifice their desire for star status in order to help the team win.

A case in point was John Schweiz, who I had first picked as the starting shooting guard. His backup was a flamboyant former NBA player named Frankie J. Sanders. (The "J," he said, stood for "Jumpshot.") Sanders had been drafted by the San Antonio Spurs and modeled himself, with limited success, after George Gervin, the team's four-time NBA scoring leader. Early in the season Schweiz came to me and suggested that I give his starter's slot to Sanders because Frankie was morose playing for the second unit. It was a completely selfless act on Schweiz's part, and, as it turned out, a masterful maneuver. Sanders led the Patroons in scoring that year, and the team took off, finishing in first place in the division. And even though he didn't get as many minutes, Schweiz, not Sanders, was called up to the NBA at the end of the season.

The identity of the team developed slowly. More often than not, it emerged in unexpected ways. Once we threw a makeshift birthday party for Rosen that had a galvanizing effect on the players. Our road trips helped, too. We spent a lot of time traveling around the Northeast in a ramshackle Dodge van—to glamorous cities such as Brockton, Massachusetts; Lancaster, Pennsylvania; and Bangor, Maine. Sometimes I'd put on the cruise control and work on crossword puzzles while I was driving. The players couldn't believe their eyes the first time I did it, and they teased me relentlessly afterwards. It was a good sign. We were starting to feel like a family.

The turning point for the team came in a playoff game against the Puerto Rico Coquis in San Juan. Playing in Puerto Rico was never easy because the crowds were raucous and the refs had no mercy on visiting teams. In this particular game, the Coquis started getting physical right away, and it looked like a fight might break out any minute. The refs seemed to be oblivious, and that enraged Rosen. Finally when a Puerto Rico player took a punch at one of our players, Charley ran out on court, flailing his arms and screaming, "If you don't stop doing that, I'm going to kick your ass."

Everybody stopped.

Rosen looked ridiculous: a tall, balding, forty-five-year-old man dressed in an ice cream suit yelling obscenities at a player half his age. The spectacle immediately dissolved the tension. That incident showed me just how effective humor can be as a catalyst for deepening team spirit.

My approach is slightly more understated than Charley's. Last year Scottie Pippen, who had been angling for weeks to be traded, made a tongue-in-cheek remark to reporters in Boston: "Trade me or trade [Jerry] Krause." That line was a banner headline in the Chicago papers the next day, and Krause called Scottie into his office to discuss it before practice. Afterwards, Scottie trudged dejectedly into the team room, where we were watching a game tape, and I said, "So, Scottie, what do you think we can get for Krause?" He laughed. The idea of trading Krause, a short, portly executive without much foot speed, for an NBA player was patently absurd. Suddenly the gloom that had been dogging the team for days lifted.

In Puerto Rico, Charley's antics led to a serious discussion about commitment after the game. I reminded the players that Rosen was getting paid almost nothing and had to come to work in a ludicrous uniform, but he was so devoted he was willing to make a fool of himself, and even risk his life, to help the team.

As we talked about the incident, the players seemed to get the message that they needed to cross the line and make a Rosenesque commitment to the cause. After that, the team spirit began to soar, and we pushed all the way to the CBA championship.

THE PRACTICE OF ACCEPTANCE

Pro basketball may be a man's world, but working with the Patroons I discovered that I was far more effective as a coach when I balanced the masculine and feminine sides of my nature. This was not an easy lesson for me. In the early years of our marriage, my wife June, who was raised in a more nurturing family than I was, would get exasperated with me when I'd display rigidity with our kids. Patiently she showed me how to temper my hard-edged aggressive instincts and become more compassionate toward myself and others—especially our children. In my case, healing the split between feminine and masculine, heart and mind—as symbolized by my compassionate father and analytic mother—has been an essential aspect of my growth both as a coach and a human being.

Though there are occasions when a firm hand is needed, I learned early that one of the most important qualities of a leader is listening without judgment, or with what Buddhists call *bare attention*. This sounds easier than it is, especially when the stakes are high and you desperately need your charges to perform. But many of the men I've coached have come from troubled families and needed all the support they could get. I find that when I can be truly present with impartial, open awareness, I get a much better feel for the players' concerns than when I try to impose my own agenda. And, paradoxically, when I back off and just listen, I get much better results on the court.

In *The Tao of Leadership*, John Heider writes:

> The wise leader is of service: receptive, yielding, follow-ing. The group member's vibration dominates and leads, while the leader follows. But soon it is the member's consciousness which is transformed. It is the job of the leader to be aware of the group member's process; it is the need of the group member to be received and paid attention to. Both get what they need, if the leader has the wisdom to serve and follow.

There's only so much a coach can do to influence the outcome of a game. If you push too hard to control what happens, resistance builds and reality spits in your face. During the 1991 playoffs, I got into a shouting match on the sidelines with Horace Grant precipitated by my stubborn insistence on playing defense a cer-tain way. Horace was having trouble guarding Armon Gilliam in a series against the Philadelphia 76ers, and he pleaded for some help with a double-team. But even though the strategy I was using wasn't working, I was adamant: I insisted that Horace play Gilliam straight up. Late in the third quarter of Game 3, Gilliam elbowed Horace, and Horace turned and hit him back. The refs called a foul on Horace, and, in a rage, I pulled him out of the game. That's when the yelling began. All of a sudden, Horace, who is devoutly religious, was cursing at me and shouting "I'm tired of being your whipping boy." Eventually, after a few more outbursts, he calmed down, but the game was lost. Clinging to a misguided notion of how things should be, I ended up alienating

Horace and making a bad judgment that ultimately cost us the game.

In Zen it is said that the gap between accepting things the way they are and wishing them to be otherwise is "the tenth of an inch of difference between heaven and hell." If we can accept whatever hand we've been dealt—no matter how unwelcome— the way to proceed eventually becomes clear. This is what is meant by right action: the capacity to observe what's happening and act appropriately, without being distracted by self-centered thoughts. If we rage and resist, our angry, fearful minds have trouble quieting down sufficiently to allow us to act in the most beneficial way for ourselves and others.

THE ART OF CHAOS

In 1984 the owner of a professional team in Quebradillas, Puerto Rico, offered me a summer job. The Superior Basketball League, whose three-month season started in June, was considered a good training ground. Red Holzman, Tex Winter, and John Bach had worked there, and so had many other NBA coaches, including K. C. Jones and Sam Jones. Three weeks after I arrived, I was fired because the team's superstar didn't like the selfless system of basketball I had implemented. However, the team owner lined up another spot for me with a far better team, the Isabela Gallitos. The Gallitos made it to the finals that year—a new high for them—and I returned for three more summers.

Coaching in Puerto Rico taught me how to cope with chaos. The games were raucous affairs, played late at night in sweltering openair arenas called conchas. The fans showed up early, often drunk, and started parading around banging bongos and tom-

toms and blowing air horns. Fights often broke out in the stands. The owner of the Quebradillas team always carried a gun with him to games in Isabela, he said, because there was "a lot of bad blood between the two towns." Once, the mayor of Quebradillas fired a gun at one of the refs during a home game because he disagreed with a call, and wounded an usher. For his sentence, he was forbidden from ever attending a game in the Roberto Clemente stadium again.

The players loved the game, and their connection with each other was stronger than on any team I've ever coached. Players rarely got traded or dumped, and there seemed to be a party every week for members of the extended family. Not all the players spoke English, and my Spanish consisted of a single word, at first, *"Defensa!"* So I had to learn how to teach and communicate nonverbally. I also had to adapt to the Puerto Rican concept of time. In Albany I had a rule that if you missed practice, you'd have to sit out the next game. If I did that in Puerto Rico, we would have had to default the whole season. Once the players were on the floor, however, they threw themselves into the game with unbridled energy. Sometimes they played in such a frenzy that all I could do was sit back and watch.

Albert Einstein once described his rules of work: "One: Out of clutter, find simplicity. Two: From discord, find harmony. Three: In the middle of difficulty lies opportunity." That was the kind of attitude I had to have working in Puerto Rico. It wasn't easy for me. I had to let go of my compulsive need for order and learn how to stay composed when everything seemed hopelessly out of control.

The key moment for me came during a game in San Germán, a town in the southwest whose fans hated the Gallitos so much they lit candles the night before we arrived and prayed for our death. Just before the game was about to start, someone broke a rim on one of the baskets, and everybody in the stadium, including about 5,000 fans, had to wait while the rim was being rewelded at the local gas station.

It took forever. Meanwhile the fans were getting drunk and restless, and the drums were beating louder and louder. My kids were running wild, and June was worried about Chelsea, whose leg was swollen from a spider bite. (Thankfully she recovered a few days later.) I tend to get phobic in large stadiums, unless I'm down on the floor, separated from the crowd. All this craziness was making me nervous, so I retreated to the dressing room to sit zazen.

It was a dank concrete room, lit by a dim bulb dangling from the ceiling. My players were so spooked by the place they always came fully dressed for games in San Germán. They never told me why; I thought it had something to do with witchcraft. After sitting in the dressing room for a while, however, I spotted the reason out of the corner of my eye: a tarantula the size of a softball crawling down the wall inches from my head.

In an attempt to escape one fear I'd come face to face with (for me) an even greater fear. Ever since childhood, I've been terrified of spiders, but my mind was clear enough at that moment so that I didn't panic. I just sat there and watched the giant tarantula slowly—ever so slowly—make its way along the wall. I wanted to sit through the fear, to experience it as fully as possible, until I felt comfortable enough to just be there in the room. And I did. When I finally got up and returned to the stadium, I didn't feel anxious anymore. From then on, the riotous nature of life in Puerto Rico no longer posed a threat.

THE HOWL OF THE EGO

Albany, however, was another matter. In 1984–85 the Patroons had the best record in the league, and I was named Coach of the Year. But a disturbing incident occurred during the playoffs that cost us a second championship and ultimately tore the team apart. Naturally, it involved Frankie Sanders.

After we won the championship in 1984, Sanders asked management for a substantial raise. The man who ran the team—Albany county executive Jim Coyne—buckled under, fearing we might lose our star attraction, and effectively abolished my equal-pay scheme. Coyne had no appreciation for the subtleties of the player-coach relationship; all he cared about was winning re-election—and keeping the Patroons on top was part of his campaign strategy.

Sanders became more audacious after he got his raise, grousing continually about how I distributed playing time. During the first round of the playoffs, against the Toronto Tornados, I got fed up and took him out of a game early. Moments later I looked down the bench and saw he'd taken off his shoes. "What are you doing?" I screamed. "Put your shoes back on."

"No," he said defiantly. "I'm going down to the locker room. My foot hurts."

"Your foot doesn't hurt. Put your shoes on. I want you back in the game."

Sanders gave me a cold look and walked off court.

Afterwards I told him I was suspending him for the next two games. We had already dropped the first two games of the series on our own court, in large part because of Sanders' selfish attitude.

Now we faced two must-win away games. I didn't want him around poisoning the team.

When we arrived in Toronto the next day, Coyne called and said he was reinstating Sanders because "we can't live without him." My gut told me this was a bad idea, but I went along with him. Coyne promised that Sanders would apologize to the team. Instead Frankie mumbled a few meaningless words, then led the team to victory with a 35-point shooting barrage. After that he was impossible to control.

The unspoken laws of basketball are strange and mysterious. When you violate them, as Sanders did in the Toronto series, you pay a price, but never in a predictable way. I felt as if I had invited disaster by caving in and letting Sanders return. After we finished off Toronto and took on the Tampa Bay Thrillers for the championship, the drama finally played itself out.

The Thrillers' coach, Bill Musselman, had packed his team with NBA veterans, and they put a lot of pressure on Sanders. At one point during the second game, Sanders stole the ball on a breakaway and, as he passed the Tampa Bay bench, yelled "Fuck you, Muss." Musselman went nuts, and later that night called Sanders in his hotel room and told him that if he did it again, he'd sic his bodyguards on him. To prove that he was serious, he brought two 300-pound professional wrestlers to the next game.

It all came down to the last seconds of the final game. We were ahead by two points with three seconds left, but the Thrillers tied the game at the buzzer and then won in overtime. It was probably the worst loss I've ever endured. But it taught me something important—above all, trust your gut. This is the first law of leadership. Once you've made your move, you have to stand by your decision and live with the consequences because your number one loyalty has to be to the team. In the case of Sanders, I compromised my principles to placate my boss, and the players picked up on my ambivalence immediately. The solidarity that had taken so long to build suddenly evaporated. Not only did we lose the series, we were lost as a team.

WHEN RIGHT ACTION MEANS CALLING IT QUITS

After that experience, I decided to split up the team and start all over again. It was time, I told the players, to get off the CBA treadmill and look for jobs in Europe, where they could make good money and not be haunted by an NBA dream wish. I thought it would be easy to find replacements, but the competition for talent had taken a nasty turn in the CBA. Musselman's success that year—winning his first of a record four straight titles— encouraged other coaches to follow his lead and stock their teams with NBA veterans. Some owners were offering players $1,000 to $1,500 a week and slipping them illegal cash bonuses on the side. Overnight what used to be a training league for young players had turned into a cutthroat business where the owners were obsessed with winning and most of the players were cynical and self-absorbed. I wondered how long I could last.

It wasn't easy practicing enlightened management in such a climate. The team I pieced together was composed primarily of CBA lifers who weren't that receptive to my experiments with communal basketball. Discipline became a chore. We weren't spending as much time together off court, in large part because we were flying to most of our games instead of taking the van.

Then Charley Rosen got a head coaching job with the Savannah Spirits, and I lost a trusted colleague, and the only person on the team that I could really talk to.

I finally lost it a few days before Christmas in 1986. At the time I was trying to figure out what to do with Michael Graham, a forward who was as naturally gifted as any player I'd seen in the CBA. He had started as a freshman for Georgetown's 1984 NCAA championship team, but he left school shortly afterwards and now was trying to make a comeback. What troubled me about him was his inability to concentrate. Every now and then he'd make a great play, but the rest of the time his mind would be floating in the stratosphere, completely unfocused. Nothing I said made any difference. Whenever I tried to talk to him, his eyes would glaze over and he'd retreat to some dark inner corner nobody could penetrate. Finally I gave up and released him.

He took it hard, but not nearly as hard as I did. Driving home that night in the rain on the New York State Thruway, all my doubts about coaching flooded my mind. Was it really worth it? Here was a kid who was born to play basketball, someone who had enough talent to be a star in the NBA, and yet despite all my sophisticated psychology, I couldn't reach him. (Actually Graham would play a few more years in the CBA, but at the time I thought I was ending his career.) Why did it have to happen this way? Why did *I* have to be the person to snuff out his basketball dream? As I pulled off at the Woodstock exit, tears were running down my face.

Talking it over with June that night, I decided to leave the Patroons at the end of the season and look for another job, perhaps even change professions. I put some feelers out around the NBA and got a lukewarm response. The Knicks flirted with me for months about a possible assistant coaching slot, but when that fell through, I began to explore other fields. The jobs I was best suited for (according to the career placement test I took) were: 1) housekeeper, 2) trail guide, 3) counselor, and 4) lawyer. Realizing I wouldn't be able to put five children through college on a trail guide's salary, I made plans to attend law school.

It looked as though my life in basketball was over. In my mind I was getting ready to move on. Then the week I filed for unemployment, Jerry Krause gave me a call.

chapter FIVE

SELFLESSNESS

IN ACTION

One finger can't lift a pebble.

—HOPI SAYING

The Bulls' owner, Jerry Reinsdorf, once told me he thought most people were motivated by one of two forces: fear or greed. That may be true, but I also think people are motivated by love. Whether they're willing to acknowledge it or not, what drives most basketball players is not the money or the adulation, but their love of the game. They live for those moments when they can lose themselves completely in the action and experience the pure joy of competition.

One of the main jobs of a coach is to reawaken that spirit so that the players can blend together effortlessly. It's often an uphill fight. The ego-driven culture of basketball, and society in general, militates against cultivating this kind of selfless action, even for members of a team whose success as individuals is tied directly to the group performance. Our society places such a high premium on individual achievement, it's easy for players to get blinded by their own self-importance and lose a sense of intercon-nectedness, the essence of teamwork.

THE WAY OF THE BULLS

When I arrived in Chicago to join the Bulls' coaching staff, I felt as if I was setting out on a strange and wonderful adventure. No longer hampered by the responsibilities of being a head coach, I was free to become a student of the game again and explore a wide range of new ideas.

The Bulls were in a state of transition. Ever since he had taken over as vice president of basketball operations in 1985, Jerry Krause had been feverishly rearranging the lineup, trying to find the right combination of players to complement Michael Jordan. A former NBA scout, Krause had been nicknamed "the Sleuth" because of his passionate desire to scout a game incognito, but he has an uncanny ability to find extraordinary prospects at small, out-of-the-way colleges where nobody else had bothered to look. Among the many stars he had drafted were Earl Monroe, Wes Unseld, Alvan Adams, Jerry Sloan, and Norm Van Lier. In his first two years running the Bulls, he had drafted power forward Charles Oakley, who would later be traded to New York for center Bill Cartwright, and acquired point guard John Paxson, a tough-minded clutch performer who would play a major role in the Bulls' drive for the championship. Krause's biggest coup, however, was landing Scottie Pippen and Horace Grant in the 1987 draft.

Scottie's rise to the NBA read like a fairy tale. The youngest of eleven children, he grew up in Hamburg, Arkansas, a sleepy rural town where his father worked in a paper mill. When Scottie was a teenager, his father was incapacitated by a stroke, and the family had to get by on his disability payments. Scottie was a respectable point guard in high school, but at only 6'1" he didn't impress the college recruiters. But his coach believed in him and talked the athletic director at University of Central Arkansas into giving him an educational grant and a job as the basketball team's equipment manager. In his sophomore year, Scottie grew four inches and began to excel, and by his senior year had become a dynamic end-to-end player, averaging 26.3 points and 10 rebounds a game. Krause picked up on him early and tried to keep it a secret. But after Scottie excelled in a series of predraft tryout games, Krause knew he would be one of the top five prospects. So he worked out a deal to flip-flop picks with Seattle in order to acquire Scottie's draft rights.

Scottie, the fifth pick overall, was the kind of athlete Krause loves. He had long arms and big hands, and the speed and leaping ability to become a first-class all-around player. What impressed me about him was his natural aptitude for the game. Scottie had a near-genius basketball IQ: he read the court extremely well, knew how to make complicated adjustments on the run and, like Jordan, seemed to have a sixth sense about what was going to happen next. In practice Scottie gravitated toward Michael, eager to see what he could learn from him. While other young players shied away from covering Michael in scrimmages to avoid being humiliated, Scottie wasn't afraid to take him on, and often did a credible job guarding him.

Horace, the tenth pick overall, also came from a rural Southern town—Sparta, Georgia—but that's where his similarity to Pippen ended. Unlike Scottie, Horace, a 6'10" power forward, took a long time learning the intricacies of the game. He had trouble concentrating at first, and often had to make up for mental lapses with his quickness and sheer athleticism. This made him vulnerable against teams like the Detroit Pistons, who devised subtle plays that took advantage of his defensive mistakes.

Horace has an identical twin brother, Harvey, who plays for the Portland Trail Blazers. They were close growing up—so close, in fact, they claimed to have had virtually identical dreams. But their rivalry became so intense playing basketball at Clemson that Harvey decided to transfer to another school. Horace and Scottie became best friends during their rookie year, and we nicknamed them Frick and Frack because they dressed alike, drove the same model car and were rarely seen apart. As a twin, Horace expected everyone on the team to be treated equally, and later criticized management publicly for giving Jordan preferential treatment. Everyone liked Horace because he was guileless and unassuming, and had a generous heart. A devout born-again Christian, he was once so moved by the professed faith of a homeless man he met in front of a church in Philadelphia that he put him up in a hotel and gave him several hundred dollars in spending money.

THE JORDAN PROBLEM

The Bulls' head coach, Doug Collins, was an energetic leader brimming with ideas who worked well with young players like Horace and Scottie. Doug was a popular sports figure in Illinois. The first Illinois State player to be named an All-American, he scored what should have been the winning foul shots in the controversial final of the 1972 Olympics, before the clock was set back and the Soviet Union snatched the win in the closing seconds. A great outside shooter, Collins was drafted by the Philadelphia 76ers, the number one pick overall, and made the All-Star team four years in a row before being slowed down by injuries. Having played alongside Julius (Dr. J) Erving, the Picasso of the slam dunk, Collins had enormous respect for what Jordan could do with the ball and was reluctant to try anything that might inhibit his creative process.

Though Collins' coaching experience was limited, he had a sharp analytical mind, and Krause hoped that, with guidance from his veteran assistants, Tex Winter and Johnny Bach, he could solve the Michael Jordan problem. This was not an easy assignment. Jordan was just coming into his own as the best all-around player in the game. The year before I arrived—Collins' first season as head coach—Jordan had averaged 37.1 points a game to win his first of seven straight scoring titles, while also becoming the first player to make 200 steals and 100 blocked shots in a season. Jordan could do things with a basketball nobody had ever seen before: he seemed to defy gravity when he went up for a shot, hanging in the air for days—sometimes weeks—as he crafted his next masterpiece. Was it merely an illusion? It didn't matter.

Whenever he touched the ball, everyone in the stadium became transfixed, wondering what he was going to do next.

The problem was that Jordan's teammates were often just as enchanted as the fans. Collins devised dozens of plays to get the rest of the team involved in the action; in fact, he had so many he was given the name Play-a-Day Collins. That helped, but when push came to shove, the other players usually faded into the background and waited for Michael to perform another miracle. Unfortunately, this mode of attack, which assistant coach Johnny Bach dubbed "the archangel offense," was so one-dimensional the better defensive teams had little difficulty shutting it down. Our nemesis, the Detroit Pistons, came up with an effective scheme called the Jordan Rules, which involved having three or more players switch off and close in on Michael whenever he made a move to the hoop. They could get away with it because none of the other Bulls posed much of a scoring threat.

How to open up the offense and make the other players more productive was a constant topic of conversation. Early on, I told the coaching staff about Red Holzman's axiom that the sign of a great player was not how much *he* scored, but how much he lifted his teammates' performance. Collins said excitedly, "You've got to tell that to Michael." I hesitated. "No, you've got to tell him right now," Collins insisted. So I searched the gym and found Michael in the weight room chatting with the players. Slightly embarrassed, I repeated Holzman's adage, saying "Doug thought you'd like hear this." I expected Michael, who could be sarcastic, to dismiss the remark as a product of basketball's stone age. But instead he thanked me and was genuinely curious about my experience with the championship Knicks.

The following season, 1988–89, Collins moved Jordan over to point guard in midseason and made Craig Hodges, one of the league's best three-point shooters, the shooting guard. The point guard's primary job is to move the ball upcourt and direct the offense. In that position Michael would have to focus more attention on creating scoring opportunities for his teammates. The switch worked pretty well at first: though Michael's average dropped to 32.5 points per game, the other players, especially Grant, Pippen, and the newly acquired Bill Cartwright, made up the difference. But the team struggled in the playoffs. Playing against Detroit in the Eastern Conference finals, Jordan had to expend so much energy running the offense he didn't have much firepower left at the end of the game. We lost the series, 4–2.

THE TAO OF BASKETBALL

The problem with making Jordan the point guard, as I saw it, was that it didn't address the real problem: the fact that the prevalent style of offense in the NBA reinforced a self-centered approach to the game. As I traveled around the league scouting other teams, I was amazed to discover that everybody was using essentially the same *modus operandi*—power basketball. Here's a typical sequence: the point guard brings the ball up and passes it inside to one of the big men, who will either make a power move to the hoop or kick the ball out to somebody on the wing after drawing a double team. The player on the wing, in turn, will either shoot, drive to the basket, or set up a screen-and-roll play. This style, an outgrowth of inner-city playground basketball, began to infiltrate the NBA in the late seventies with the emergence of Dr. J and other spectacular open-floor players. By the late eighties, it had taken over the league. Yet, though it can inspire breathtaking flights of creativity, the action often becomes stagnant and predictable because, at any given moment, only two or three players are involved in the play. Not only does this make the game a mind-numbing experience for players who aren't big scorers, it also misleads everyone into thinking that basketball is nothing more than a sophisticated slam dunk competition.

The answer, in Tex Winter's mind, was a continuous-motion offense involving everybody on the floor. Tex, a white-haired "professor" of basketball who had played under legendary coach Sam Berry at the University of Southern California, had made a name for himself in the 1950s when he turned little-known Kansas State into a national powerhouse using a system he'd developed, then known as the triple-post offense. Jerry Krause, who was then a scout, considered Tex a genius and spent a lot of time hanging out at Kansas State practices trying to see what he could absorb. The day after he was put in charge of the Bulls, Jerry called Tex, who had recently retired from a consulting job at LSU, and coaxed him into moving to Chicago to help rebuild the franchise.

Collins had decided against using Tex's system because he thought it was better suited for college than the pros. He wasn't alone. Even Tex had his doubts. He had tried to implement it as head coach of the Houston Rockets in the early seventies without much luck. Nevertheless, the more I learned about Tex's system—which he now calls the triangle offense—the more convinced I became that it made sense for the Bulls. The Bulls weren't a big, powerful team; nor did they have a dominant point guard like Magic Johnson or Isiah Thomas. If they were going to win the championship, it was going to be with speed, quickness, and finesse. The system would allow them to do that.

Listening to Tex describe his brainchild, I realized that this was the missing link I had been searching for in the CBA. It was a more evolved version of the offense we'd run on the Knicks under Red Holzman, and, more to the point, it embodied the Zen Christian attitude of selfless awareness. In essence, the system was a vehicle for integrating mind and body, sport and spirit in a practical, down-to-earth form that anyone could learn. It was awareness in action.

The triangle offense is best described as *five-man tai chi*. The basic idea is to orchestrate the flow of movement in order to lure the defense off balance and create a myriad of openings on the floor. The system gets its name from one of the most common patterns of movement: the sideline triangle. Example: As Scottie Pippen moves the ball upcourt, he and two other players form a triangle on the right side of the floor about fifteen feet apart from each other—Steve Kerr in the corner, Luc Longley in the post and Scottie along the sideline. Meanwhile, Michael Jordan hovers around the top of the key and Toni Kukoc positions himself opposite Pippen on the other side of the floor. Next Pippen passes the ball into Longley, and everybody goes into a series of complex coordinated moves, depending on how the defense responds.

The point is not to go head-to-head with the defense, but to toy with the defenders and trick them into overextending themselves. That means thinking and moving in unison as a group and being acutely aware, at any given moment, of what's happening on the floor. Executed properly, the system is virtually unstoppable because there are no set plays and the defense can't predict what's going to happen next. If the defense tries to prevent one move, the players will adjust instinctively and start another series of cuts and passes that often lead to a better shot.

At the heart of the system are what Tex calls the seven principles of a sound offense:

1. The offense must penetrate the defense. In order to run the system, the first step is to break through the perimeter of the defense, usually around the three-point line, with a drive, a pass, or a shot. The number-one option is to pass the ball into the post and go for a three-point power play.

2. The offense must involve a full-court game. Transition offense starts on defense. The players must be able to play end-to-end and perform skills at fast-break pace.

3. The offense must provide proper spacing. This is critical. As they move around the court, the players should maintain a distance of fifteen to eighteen feet from one another. That gives everybody room to operate and prevents the defense from being able to cover two players with one man.

4. The offense must ensure player and ball movement with a purpose. All things being equal, each player will spend around eighty percent of his time *without the ball*. In the triangle offense, the players have prescribed routes to follow in those situations, so that they're all moving in harmony toward a common goal. When Toni Kukoc joined the Bulls, he tended to gravitate toward the ball when it wasn't in his hands. Now he has learned to fan away from the ball and move to the open spots—making him a much more difficult player to guard.

5. The offense must provide strong rebounding position and good defensive balance on all shots. With the triangle offense, everyone knows where to go when a shot goes up to put themselves in a position to pick off the rebound or protect against the fast break. Location is everything, especially when playing the boards.

6. The offense must give the player with the ball an opportunity to pass the ball to any of his teammates. The players move in such a way so that the ballhandler can see them and hit them with a pass. That sets up the counterpoint effect. As the defense increases the pressure on one point on the floor, an opening is inevitably created somewhere else that the defenders can't see. If the players are lined up properly, the ballhandler should be able to find someone in that spot.

7. *The offense must utilize the players' individual skills.* The system requires everybody to become an offensive threat. That means they have to find what they do best within the context of the team. As John Paxson puts it, "You can find a way to fit into the offense, no matter what your strengths are. I wasn't a creative player. I wasn't going to take the ball and beat the other guys to the basket. But I was a good shooter, and the system played to my strength. It helped me understand what I did well and find the areas on the court where I could thrive."

SURRENDERING THE "ME" FOR THE "WE"

What appealed to me about the system was that it empowered everybody on the team by making them more involved in the offense, and demanded that they put their individual needs second to those of the group. This is the struggle every leader faces: how to get members of the team who are driven by the quest for individual glory to give themselves over wholeheartedly to the group effort. In other words, how to teach them selflessness.

In basketball, this is an especially tricky problem. Today's NBA players have a dazzling array of individual moves, most of which they've learned from coaches who encourage one-on-one play. In an effort to become "stars," young players will do almost anything to draw attention to themselves, to say "This is me" with the ball, rather than share the limelight with others. The skewed reward system in the NBA only makes matters worse. Superstars with dramatic, eye-catching moves are paid vast sums of money, while players who contribute to the team effort in less flamboyant ways often make close to the minimum salary. As a result, few players come to the NBA dreaming of becoming good team players. Even players who weren't standouts in college believe that once they hit the pros somehow the butterfly will emerge from the chrysalis. This is a hard one to refute because there are several players around the league who've come out of nowhere to find stardom.

The battle for players' minds begins at an early age. Most talented players start getting special treatment in junior high school, and by the time they reach the pros, they've had eight years or more of being coddled. They have NBA general managers, sporting goods manufacturers, and assorted hucksters dangling money in front of them and an entourage of agents, lawyers, friends, and family members vying for their favor. Then there's the media, which can be the most alluring temptress of all. With so many people telling them how great they are, it's difficult, and, in some cases, impossible, for coaches to get players to check their inflated egos at the gym door.

Tex's system helps undo some of this conditioning by getting players to play basketball with a capital B instead of indulging their self-interest. The principles of the system are the code of honor that everybody on the team has to live by. We put them on the chalkboard and talk about them almost every day. The principles serve as a mirror that shows each player how well they're doing with respect to the team mission.

The relationship between a coach and his players is often fraught with tension because the coach is constantly critiquing each player's performance and trying to get him to change his behavior. Having a clearly defined set of principles to work with reduces conflict because it depersonalizes the criticism. The players understand that you're not attacking them personally when you correct a mistake, but only trying to improve their knowledge of the system.

Learning that system is a demanding, often tedious process that takes years to master. The key is a repetitive series of drills that train the players, on an experiential level as well as an intellectual one, to move, as Tex puts it, "like five fingers on a hand." In that respect, the drills resemble Zen practice. After months of focusing intently on performing the drills in practice, the players begin to see—Aha! This is how all the pieces fit together. They develop an intuitive feel for how their movements and those of everyone else on the floor are interconnected.

Not everyone reaches this point. Some players' self-centered conditioning is so deeply rooted they can't make that leap. But for those who can, a subtle shift in consciousness occurs. The beauty of the system is that it allows players to experience another, more powerful form of motivation than ego-gratification. Most rookies arrive in the NBA thinking that what will make them happy is having unlimited freedom to strut their egos on national TV. But that approach to the game is an inherently empty experience. What makes basketball so exhilarating is the joy of losing yourself completely in the dance, even if it's just for one beautiful transcendent moment. That's what the system teaches players. There's a lot of freedom built into the process, but it's the freedom that John Paxson talks about, the freedom of shaping a role for yourself and using all of your creative resources to work in unison with others.

When I started coaching, Dick Motta, a veteran NBA coach, told me that the most important part of the job takes place on the practice floor, not during the game. After a certain point you have to trust the players to translate into action what they've learned in practice. Using a comprehensive system of basketball makes it easier for me to detach myself in that way. Once the players have mastered the system, a powerful group intelligence emerges that is greater than the coach's ideas or those of any individual on the team. When a team reaches that state, the coach can step back and let the game itself "motivate" the players. You don't have to give them any "win one for the Gipper" pep talks; you just have to turn them loose and let them immerse themselves in the action.

During my playing days, the Knicks had that kind of feeling. Everyone loved playing with each other so much, we had an unspoken rule among ourselves about not skipping games, no matter what your excuse. Some players—Willis Reed was the most famous example—refused to sit out even when they could barely walk. What did pain matter? We didn't want to miss the dance.

EASY RIDER

As it turned out, I got a chance to experiment with the triangle offense sooner than I expected. Toward the end of the 1988–89 season, the team went into a slide, and even though we made it to the conference finals, Jerry Krause lost faith in Doug Collins' ability to push the team to the next level and decided to let him go.

The portrait the press has painted of Jerry over the years is not very flattering. He is extremely distrustful of reporters, having been burned by them in the past, and is so secretive that distortions inevitably occur. (In 1991, when *The Jordan Rules*—a book by Chicago *Tribune* writer Sam Smith that portrayed Krause as hard-headed, insensitive, and a bit of a schlemiel—came out, Jerry called me into his office and pointed out 176 "lies" he'd discovered in it.)

Jerry and I are bipolar opposites. He's circumspect with the press; I'm overly trusting. He's nervous and compulsive; I'm laid-back to the point of being almost comatose. We are both strong-willed and have had several flaming arguments over what to do with the team. Jerry encourages dissent, not just from me, but from everybody on the staff. But when he finally sits down to make a decision, he keeps his own counsel, a habit he developed as a scout.

Jerry loves to tell the story of Joe Mason, a former scout for the New York Mets. Several years ago, when Jerry was director of scouting for the Chicago White Sox, he noticed that Mason had a knack for finding great prospects that nobody else knew about. When Jerry asked his scouts what Mason's secret was, they said he always ate alone and never shared information with anybody else. In other words, he was like Jerry Krause.

Jerry's unorthodox style of management worked to my advantage. The NBA is a small exclusive club that's extremely difficult to break into as a coach unless you're connected with one of its four or five major cliques. Even though I had won a championship and been named Coach of the Year in the CBA, nobody was willing to take a chance on me except Krause. He didn't care about my overblown reputation as a sixties flower child. All he wanted to know was whether I could help turn his team into a champion.

I must have passed the test. Jerry and I had worked together on the Bill Cartwright–Charles Oakley trade, and he was impressed by my ability to judge character. He also liked the fact that I had taken such a keen interest in the triangle offense, though he assured me that implementing it wouldn't be a job requirement. Several days after he dismissed Collins, Jerry called me in Montana to offer me the head coaching job.

We had a party line then, and, in true Krausian fashion, he asked me to go to a more secure phone, at a gas station six miles away. After we finished talking, I jumped on my BMW motorcycle and headed back to the lake. My mind was racing as fast as the engine as I sped down the road. "Now that I'm a head coach," I said to myself, easing off the throttle, "I guess I can't take risks and be so outrageous."

I thought that one over for a second and laughed. Then I gunned the bike all the way home.

chapter SIX

THE EYE

OF BASKETBALL

Dreams are wiser than men.
—OMAHA SAYING

Call me Swift Eagle. That's the name Edgar Red Cloud gave me during the 1973 basketball clinic that Bill Bradley and I conducted at the Pine Ridge Reservation in South Dakota. Edgar, the grandson of the famous chief Red Cloud, said I resembled an eagle as I swooped around the court with my arms outstretched, always looking to steal the ball. Swift Eagle. *Ohnahkoh Wamblee*. The name sounded like wings beating the air.

The elders of the tribe performed a naming ceremony for Bill and me in the high school gym. I found it amusing that the Lakota always gave outsiders exalted names—Bill's was Tall Elk—while their own people had to settle for ones like Stinking

Dog and Lame Deer. But I was honored by my name, and, in a funny way, it fit.

To Lakota warriors, the eagle is the most sacred of birds because of its vision and its role as a messenger to the Great Spirit. The famed Lakota holy man, Black Elk, painted a spotted eagle on his horse before going into battle to strengthen his eagle medicine. As a young boy, inflicted with a terminal illness, he had a vision detailed in his book, *Black Elk Speaks*, of leaving his body and flying, like an eagle, to the "high and lonely center of the earth," where he saw "the shapes of all things in the spirit" and understood that "the sacred hoop of my people was one of many hoops that made one circle." Empowered by his vision, Black Elk recovered his health and grew into a warrior with exceptional mystical gifts.

Maybe Edgar Red Cloud had been gazing into the future when he gave me my new name. According to Jamie Sams and David Carson, authors of *Medicine Cards*, a book of Native American myths, the eagle represents "a state of grace achieved through hard work, understanding, and a completion of the tests of initiation which result in the taking of one's personal power."

My initiation, it seemed, was finally over.

THE EAGLE'S VIEW

My first act after being named head coach of the Bulls was to formulate a vision for the team. I had learned from the Lakota and my own experience as a coach that vision is the source of leadership, the expansive dream state where everything begins and all is possible. I started by creating a vivid picture in my mind of what the team could become. My vision could be lofty,

I reminded myself, but it couldn't be a pipe dream. I had to take into account not only *what* I wanted to achieve, but *how* I was going to get there.

At the heart of my vision was the selfless ideal of teamwork that I'd been experimenting with since my early days in the CBA. My goal was to give everyone on the team a vital role—even though I knew I couldn't give every man equal playing time, nor could I change the NBA's disproportionate system of financial rewards. But I could get the bench players to be more actively involved. My idea was to use ten players regularly and give the others enough playing time so that they could blend in effortlessly with everybody else when they were on the floor. I've often been criticized for leaving backups on the floor too long, but I think the cohesion it creates is more than worth the gamble. In Game 6 of the 1992 finals against the Portland Trail Blazers, we were down by 17 points in the third quarter and sinking fast. So I put in the second unit. The rest of the coaching staff, not to mention members of the press, thought I'd finally gone over the edge, but within minutes the subs wiped out the deficit and put us back in the game.

Tex Winter's system would be my blueprint. But that alone wasn't going to be enough. We needed to reinforce the lessons the players were learning in practice, to get them to embrace the concept of selflessness wholeheartedly.

FISH DON'T FLY

When a fish swims in the ocean, there is no limit to the water, no matter how far it swims.
When a bird flies in the sky, there is no limit to the air,

no matter how far it flies.
However, no fish or bird has ever left its element since
the beginning.

This ancient Zen teaching holds great wisdom for anyone envisioning how to get the most out of a group. Just as fish don't fly and elephants don't play rock and roll, you can't expect a team to perform in a way that's out of tune with its basic abilities. Though the eagle may soar and fly close to the heavens, its view of the earth is broad and unclouded. In other words, you can dream all you want, but, bottom line, you've got to work with what you've got. Otherwise, you're wasting your time. The team won't buy your plan and everyone—most of all you—will end up frustrated and disappointed. But when your vision is based on a clear-sighted, realistic assessment of your resources, alchemy often mysteriously occurs and a team transforms into a force greater than the sum of its individual talents. Inevitably, paradoxically, the acceptance of boundaries and limits is the gateway to freedom.

But visions are never the sole property of one man or one woman. Before a vision can become reality, it must be owned by every single member of the group.

If I was going to have any success realizing my vision for the team, I knew my first challenge was to win over Michael Jordan. He was the team leader, and the other players would follow if he went along with the program. Michael and I had a good rapport, but I wasn't certain how he would respond to the idea of giving up the ball and taking fewer shots. Usually coaches have to coax their star to produce more; in a way, I was asking Michael to produce less. How much less, I wasn't sure. Perhaps enough to prevent him from winning his fourth straight scoring title. Scoring champions rarely play for championship teams because during the playoffs the best teams tighten their defenses and can shut down a great shooter, as Detroit had done with Michael, by double- and triple-teaming him. The last player to win the scoring crown and a championship in the same year had been Kareem Abdul-Jabbar in 1971.

Michael was more receptive than I thought he would be. Right after Labor Day we had a private meeting in my office, and I told him, "You've got to share the spotlight with your teammates because if you don't, they won't grow."

"Does that mean we're going to use Tex's equal opportunity offense?" he asked.

"Yes, I think so."

"Well, I think we're going to have trouble when the ball gets to certain people," he said, "because they can't pass and they can't make decisions with the ball." In particular, he was concerned about Horace Grant, who had trouble thinking on his feet, and Bill Cartwright, who was so unsure with his hands that Michael jokingly accused him of eating Butterfinger candy bars before practice.

"I understand that," I replied. "But I think if you give the system a chance, they'll learn to be playmakers. The important thing is to let everybody touch the ball, so they won't feel like spectators. You can't beat a good defensive team with one man. It's got to be a team effort."

"Okay, you know me. I've always been a coachable player. Whatever you want to do, I'm behind you."

That was it. From then on, Michael devoted himself to learning the system and finding a way to make it work for him. He was never a total convert, but he liked the fact that defenses would have a harder time double- and triple-teaming him. Once we started using the triangle offense in games, what surprised

me was how much havoc Michael could create moving *without
the ball*. Defenders couldn't take their minds off him, as he wove
his way around the floor. Just the thought that he might get the
ball at any moment was enough to spook opponents into giving
up easy shots.

One of the obstacles we had to overcome was the players'
dependency on Michael. It was almost an addiction. In pressure
situations, they kept looking to him to bail them out. I kept
telling them that if they learned to fake to Michael and go the
other way, shots would open up and it would take pressure off
him to always make the big plays. Every now and then Michael
would break loose and take over a game. But that didn't bother
me as long as it didn't become a habit. I knew he needed bursts
of creativity to keep from getting bored, and that his solo performances would strike terror in the hearts of our enemies, not to
mention help win some key games.

At first, Michael had doubts that the triangle offense was
suitable for the pros, primarily because it took so long to learn
and practice time was limited. As it was, a year and half went by
before the team was entirely comfortable with it, and Michael
estimates it was another two and a half years before everyone
mastered its many nuances. "To this day, I still make mistakes
with it," he says. When Michael returned to the team in 1995,
he had a deeper appreciation of the system. It allowed him to fit
smoothly into the flow of the offense, though some of his teammates had trouble adjusting to his presence on the floor. They'd
either stop in their tracks when he got the ball, expecting him
to make one of his creative moves, or get so caught up in cutting
to their spots they'd block his path to the basket.

In Michael's mind, the system is basically a three-quarter
offense. "The triangle gets us to the fourth quarter," he says.

"Then it's a whole different game." But, he adds, thinking back to the championship team, "in the fourth quarter Bill was in the post; Scottie and I were in open court; B. J. Armstrong or Paxson was on the wing; and Horace was on the boards. With the talent and *think power* we had, we were able to open up the court and let one or two guys penetrate, then feed off of them. In the fourth quarter your leadership, your unity, your understanding of personnel, your fulfillment of roles—all those things come out. And I think that's the way we won."

I wouldn't disagree with him. In fact, that was part of my vision, for the players to expand the strategy and make it their own. The system was the starting point. Without it, they would never have developed the "think power" Michael talks about or learned to create something as a group that transcended the limits of their own singular imaginations.

BUILDING CONSENSUS

Another important step I took to consolidate the team was to name Cartwright cocaptain. I had played against Bill in the late seventies and knew he had natural leadership abilities. Jordan was a good on-court leader and handled the media skillfully, but I sensed that Bill would be a better leader in the locker room, helping players cope with frustration and disappointment. He was a master at listening without judgment. An NBA team is a highly charged environment, and players are always grumbling about something, no matter how compassionate the coach is or how well the team is doing. Bill was adept at deflecting that anger by giving his teammates a chance to air their complaints. When Cartwright was starting out with the Knicks, he injured his foot and was so depressed he came close to quitting. But veteran Louis Orr listened patiently, then persuaded him to stick it out. Bill had never forgotten that lesson.

Naming Cartwright cocaptain made the team less Jordan-centric. Bill and Michael weren't best friends. In fact, Michael wasn't convinced, at first, that trading Charles Oakley, his best friend on the team, for Cartwright was such a smart idea. But Bill wasn't intimidated by Jordan and, in his low-key, dignified way, he showed the younger players that they didn't have to kowtow to Michael all the time. Jordan changed his opinion of Bill when he saw how strong he was on defense. Cartwright wasn't afraid to put his 7'1", 245-lb. body on the line, day in and day out, no matter how injured he was or who he was guarding. Once I ran a drill in practice that pitted the guards against the centers. When Michael went one-on-one against Cartwright, Bill had such a fierce look in his eyes a silence fell over the room. Cartwright bumped Michael as he went up and sent him flying horizontally through the air. It was a chilling experience for Jordan, even though Bill cushioned his fall. Needless to say, I didn't use that drill again that year.

We call Bill the "Protector" because he is our last line of defense. Other players could take chances going for steals and blocking shots because they could count on Cartwright to cover for them and keep them from being embarrassed. "If a guy beat me," said Jordan, "he knew he'd have to get by Bill to reach the basket. So more than likely he'd pull back and try to make a jump shot. When that's in the back of your mind, it really helps your defense."

At thirty-two, Bill was the oldest player on the team, and his soft whispery voice and salt-and-pepper goatee gave him a quiet professorial demeanor. The players nicknamed him Teach and marveled at his ability to dominate bigger, stronger, quicker centers. "Bill would meet each center at the three-point line and start banging them," remembers guard Craig Hodges. "By the time they got to what they thought was the post, they would still be way outside, and that's where we wanted them. He would make Patrick Ewing work so hard for every shot; it was truly an art form. He took all the centers out of their games. It was like the teacher's in the house. 'Teach' is holding class."

Cartwright knew exactly what I was trying to do, sometimes even better than I did, and could explain it to the younger players in a non-threatening way. He helped me turn them into dreamers, to expand their vision of what they could become.

EMPOWERING THE TEAM

At the core of my vision was getting the players to think more for themselves. Doug Collins had kept the younger players, especially Scottie Pippen and Horace Grant, on a tight rein, frequently yelling at them when they made mistakes. Throughout the game they'd look over at the bench, nervously trying to read his mind. When they started doing that with me, I immediately cut them off. "Why are you looking at me?" I'd ask. "You already know you made a mistake."

If the players were going to learn the offense, they would have to have the confidence to make decisions on their own. That would never happen if they were constantly searching for direction from me. I wanted them to *dis*connect themselves from me, so they could connect with their teammates—and the game.

Having Jordan on the floor helped. He'd often call the team

together for a few seconds in the middle of a game to give the younger players an impromptu tutorial. That kind of on-the-job problem-solving was invaluable not only because it speeded up the learning process, but also because it strengthened the group mind. Some coaches feel threatened when their players start asserting their independence, but I think it's much more effective to open up the decision-making process to everybody. Each game is a riddle that must be solved, and there are no textbook answers. The players often have a better handle on the problem than the coaching staff because they're right in the thick of the action and can pick up intuitively the opposition's strengths and weaknesses.

To reach that point I had to give the players the freedom to find out what worked and what didn't. That meant putting them out on the floor together in unusual combinations and letting them deal with treacherous situations without bailing them out. Some players found this to be a maddening ordeal. B. J. Armstrong, a rookie point guard from the University of Iowa in 1989–90, was perplexed when I left him in games for long stretches even though none of his shots were going in. I wanted to teach him that shooting wasn't the only thing that mattered. Defense was far more important. Eventually he got the message and developed a broader view of what he could do for the team.

B.J. had trouble adapting to the system at first because, like most young players, his personal agenda was clouding his mind. Every time he got the ball he wanted to show the world what he could do—to score, to make a spectacular assist, to get back at his man for humiliating him on the last play. A 6′2″ veteran of Detroit's inner-city playgrounds, he was fixated on attacking the hoop like his boyhood idol, Isiah Thomas. That kind of thinking was counterproductive because it took him out of the moment and diminished his awareness of what the team was doing as a whole. It also telegraphed to the defense what he was going to do. When B.J. tried to muscle his way to the basket through a swarm of giants, he looked like a man on a suicide mission. The defenders would often knock him down, strip the ball away, and score a quick basket at the other end while he was still getting up from the floor.

CELLULOID DREAMS

Being in tune with what's happening on court and fitting into the flow of action is far more important than trying to be heroic. "You don't always have to be the one who takes the shot down the stretch," I tell players. "Don't force it. Let it happen to whoever is open."

Sometimes I drive this point home with movie clips. One night mulling over an upcoming game against Detroit, I came up with the idea of using *The Wizard of Oz* as a teaching device. The Pistons had been waging psychological warfare against us—and winning. I needed to turn the tables by making the players aware of how Detroit's roughneck style of play was affecting the team as a whole. So I mixed vignettes from *The Wizard of Oz* with clips from Pistons games for our next tape session.

This is a trick I learned from assistant coach Johnny Bach. Basketball players spend an inordinate amount of time watching videotapes, which can be a tense, embarrassing experience—especially when their teammates start ribbing them about their mistakes. Bach, a witty ex-Navy man who viewed basketball as a war game, subtly indoctrinated the players by splicing clips from movies such as *An Officer and a Gentleman* and *Full Metal Jacket* into the game tapes. The results were often quite funny.

The *Wizard of Oz* tape was a hit, too. One sequence showed B.J. dribbling to the basket and being flattened by the Detroit front line, followed by a shot of Dorothy arriving in the Land of Oz, looking around and saying to her faithful dog, "This isn't Kansas anymore, Toto." B.J. laughed. The message? You're not playing against college players anymore; you're playing against hardened professionals, who'll stomp all over you if you give them half a chance. Another sequence showed Horace Grant, who needed to develop court savvy, being faked out by Isiah Thomas on a screen-and-roll play, followed by the Scarecrow talking about how great it would be to have a brain. In one way or another, the tape poked fun at everyone on the team. That was important. I didn't want to single out any one person for criticism. As far as I was concerned, they all needed to be smarter, more alert, and less intimidated by the Pistons' back-alley tactics.

THE WAY OF THE WARRIOR

The system taught the mechanics, but to create the kind of cohesive team I envisioned, I needed to touch the players on a much deeper level. I wanted to give them a model of selfless action that would capture their imaginations.

Enter the Lakota Sioux.

The basketball clinic Bill Bradley and I gave at Pine Ridge in 1973 was part of a six-year series I organized with some Lakota friends to give the community something to focus on other than politics. The first clinic, which also included Willis Reed, took place in the summer of 1973, a few months after the American Indian Movement's widely publicized protest at Wounded Knee.

Working with the Lakota children, who had an intense passion for the sport, I became fascinated by Sioux culture and its proud warrior heritage.

Lakota warriors had a deep reverence for the mysteries of life. That's where their power, and sense of freedom, came from. It was no coincidence that Crazy Horse, the greatest Sioux warrior, was first and foremost a holy man. To the Lakota, everything was sacred, even the enemy, because of their belief in the interconnectedness of all life. As one seer put it: "We are earth people on a spiritual journey to the stars. Our quest, our earth walk, is to look within, to know who we are, to see that we are connected to all things, that there is no separation, only in the mind."

The Lakota didn't perceive of the self as a separate entity, isolated from the rest of the universe. The stones they carved into arrowheads, the buffalo they hunted, the Crow warriors they battled, were all seen as reflections of themselves. Black Elk wrote in *The Sacred Pipe*, "Peace . . . comes within the souls of men when they realize their relationship, their oneness with the universe and all its powers, and when they realize that at the center of the Universe dwells the Great Spirit, and that this center is really everywhere. It is within each of us."

The Lakotas' concept of teamwork was deeply rooted in their view of the universe. A warrior didn't try to stand out from his fellow band members; he strove to act bravely and honorably, to help the group in whatever way he could to accomplish its mission. If glory befell him, he was obligated to give away his most prized possessions to relatives, friends, the poor, and the aged. As a result, the leaders of the tribe were often its poorest members. A few years ago I received a beautiful handwoven blanket from a Sioux woman in North Dakota who said her brother had broken the state championship scoring record I had set in the 1960s. His achievement had brought so much honor to her family, she thought it only fitting to send me a gift.

It struck me that the Lakota way could serve as a paradigm for the Bulls because there were so many parallels between the warrior's journey and life in the NBA. A basketball team is like a band of warriors, a secret society with rites of initiation, a strict code of honor, and a sacred quest—the drive for the championship trophy. For Lakota warriors, life was a fascinating game. They would trek across half of Montana, enduring untold hardships, for the thrill of sneaking into an enemy camp and making off with a string of ponies. It wasn't the ponies per se that mattered so much, but the experience of pulling off something difficult together as a team. NBA players get the same feeling when they fly into an unfriendly city and steal away with a big win.

THE MYSTIC WARRIOR

My first lecture to the players on the Lakota ideal began as a way to poke fun at Johnny Bach. Johnny and I were both assistant coaches at the time, and he was giving the players a daily diet of his unique brand of blood-and-guts psychology. Bach, who had a long career as a head coach in college and the pros before joining the Bulls, liked to quote sayings from his mentor, Vince Lombardi. But compared to Johnny, Lombardi was a wimp. An energetic, young sixty-something, Bach was always the first person into the fray when a fight broke out on the floor. The players admired him because he was as tough as iron and steadfastly loyal. Johnny often showed up for games dressed in a suit with creases sewn into his pants, spit-shined shoes, and a floor-length military coat. On his wrist he wore the Navy wings of his twin brother, a pilot who had been shot down and killed during World War II.

With Johnny, you could never tell how much of his "kill or be killed" philosophy was mere bluster, but the players loved it. In the dressing room before games, he'd bark like a Paris Island drill sergeant, "Let God count the dead" or "Blood, blood, blood! We want blood!" And he'd draw an ace of spades on the chalkboard when somebody knocked his man out of the game. He got the idea after reading that American soldiers in Vietnam used to place an ace of spades on the bodies of Vietcong they'd slain. I decided to counter with some propaganda of my own. I already had a reputation for being a pacifist—when I'd shown up for practice one day sporting a Grateful Dead T-shirt, one of the beat writers had done a story portraying me as the team's resident peacenik. So to tweak Johnny, I often livened up game tapes I edited with clips of Jimi Hendrix playing the national anthem at Woodstock or David Byrne's video of "Once in a Lifetime"—a song about the importance of being in the moment. And I found that many of the players appreciated this approach because it was such a departure from the typical coach's routine.

Around this time I also discovered *The Mystic Warrior*, a made-for-TV movie based on Ruth Beebe Hill's novel *Hanta Yo*. It tells the story of a young Sioux warrior, loosely based on Crazy Horse, who has a powerful vision and becomes a spiritual leader. My friends at Pine Ridge dismissed the film, pointing out the inaccuracies in it. But it sharply illustrated the importance of making personal sacrifices for the good of the group, a point I thought the players needed to learn.

During the 1989 playoffs, Johnny and I put together a film session for the players to prepare them for their upcoming slugfest with the Pistons. After Johnny did his kill-and-maim number, I showed them a tape that included clips from *The Mystic Warrior*. Afterwards we talked about *hanta yo*, the Lakota war chant, which means "the spirit goes ahead of us." It was the warrior's way of saying he was totally at peace with himself as he rode into battle, ready to die, if necessary. The phrase reminded me of my former teammate John Lee Williamson's rallying cry. "Go down as you live," he would shout before games, meaning, "Don't hold back. Play the way you live your life, with your whole heart and soul."

I was encouraged by the players' enthusiastic response to these ideas. This was something I could build on, a way to talk about the spiritual aspects of basketball without sounding like a Sunday preacher. Over the next few years, I quietly integrated Lakota teachings into our program. We decorated the team room with Native American totems. We started and ended each practice in a circle to symbolize that we were forming our own sacred hoop. We even joked with Jerry Krause about replacing the bull on the teams logo with a white buffalo.

Slowly the group mind was starting to form.

chapter SEVEN

BEING AWARE IS MORE

IMPORTANT THAN

BEING SMART

*If your mind isn't clouded by unnecessary
things, this is the best season of your life.*

—WU-MEN

Basketball is a complex dance that requires shifting from one objective to another at lightning speed. To excel, you need to act with a clear mind and be totally focused on what *everyone* on the floor is doing. Some athletes describe this quality of mind as a "cocoon of concentration." But that implies shutting out the world when what you really need to do is become more acutely aware of what's happening right now, *this very moment.*

The secret is *not thinking.* That doesn't mean being stupid; it means quieting the endless jabbering of thoughts so that your body can do instinctively what it's been trained to do without the mind getting in the way. All of us have had flashes of this sense of oneness—making love, creating a work of art—when we're completely immersed in the moment, inseparable from what we're doing. This kind of experience happens all the time on the basketball floor; that's why the game is so intoxicating. But if you're really paying attention, it can also occur while you're performing the most mundane tasks. In *Zen and the Art of Motorcycle Maintenance*, Robert Pirsig writes about cultivating "the peace of mind which does not separate one's self from one's surroundings" while working on his bike. "When that is done successfully," he writes, "then everything else follows naturally. Peace of mind produces right values, right values produce right thoughts. Right thoughts produce right actions and right actions produce work which will be a material reflection for others to see of the serenity at the center of it all." This is the essence of what we try to cultivate in our players.

In Zen it is said that all you need to do to reach enlightenment is "chop wood, carry water." The point is to perform every activity, from playing basketball to taking out the garbage, with precise attention, moment by moment. This idea became a focus for me while I was visiting my brother Joe's commune in Taos, New Mexico, in the late seventies. One day I noticed a banner flying near the dining hall that read simply "Remember." It made such an impression on me that I hung a replica of the flag outside my home in Montana. Now, faded and weather-beaten, it still calls out for total attention.

For some people, notably Michael Jordan, the only impetus they need to become completely focused is intense competition. But for most of us, athletes and nonathletes alike, the battle itself is not enough. Many of the players I've worked with tend to *lose* their equanimity after a certain point as the level of competition rises, because their minds start racing out of control.

When I was a player, not surprisingly, my biggest obstacle was my hyperactive critical mind. I'd been trained by my Pentecostal parents to stand guard over my thoughts, meticulously sorting out the "pure" from the "impure." That kind of intense judgmental thinking—*this* is good, *that's* bad—is not unlike the mental process most professional athletes go through every day. Everything they've done since junior high school has been dissected, analyzed, measured, and thrown back in their faces by their coaches, and, in many cases, the media. By the time they reach the pros, the inner critic rules. With the precision of a cuckoo clock, he crops up whenever they make a mistake. *How did that guy beat me? Where did that shot come from? What a stupid pass!* The incessant accusations of the judging mind block vital energy and sabotage concentration.

Some NBA coaches exacerbate the problem by rating every move players make with a plus-minus system that goes far beyond conventional statistics. "Good" moves—fighting for position, finding the open man—earn the player plus points, while "bad" moves—losing your man, fudging your footwork—show up as debits. The problem is: a player can make an important contribution to the game and still walk away with a negative score.

That approach would have been disastrous for a hypercritical player like me. That's why I don't use it. Instead, we show players how to quiet the judging mind and focus on what needs to be done at any given moment. There are several ways we do that. One is by teaching the players meditation so they can experience stillness of mind in a low-pressure setting off the court.

VENTURING INTO THE HERE
AND NOW

The meditation practice we teach players is called *mindfulness*.
To become mindful, one must cultivate what Suzuki Roshi calls
"beginner's mind," an "empty" state free from limiting self-
centered thoughts. "If your mind is empty," he writes in *Zen
Mind, Beginner's Mind*, "it is always ready for anything; it is open
to everything. In the beginner's mind there are many possibilities;
in the expert's mind there are few."

When I was coaching in Albany, Charley Rosen and I used
to give a workshop called "Beyond Basketball" at the Omega
Institute in Rhinebeck, New York. The workshop served as a
laboratory where I could experiment with a number of spiritual
and psychological practices I'd been itching to try in combination
with basketball. Part of the program involved mindfulness meditation, and it worked so well I decided to use it with the Bulls.

We started slowly. Before tape sessions, I'd turn down the
lights and lead the players through a short meditation to put
them in the right frame of mind. Later I invited George Mumford,
a meditation instructor, to give the players a three-day mindfulness course during training camp. Mumford is a colleague of
Jon Kabat-Zinn, executive director of the Center for Mindfulness
in Medicine at the University of Massachusetts Medical Center,
who has had remarkable results teaching meditation to people
coping with illness and chronic pain.

Here's the basic approach Mumford taught the players: Sit
in a chair with your spine straight and your eyes downcast. Focus
your attention on your breath as it rises and falls. When your
mind wanders (which it will, repeatedly), note the source of the

distraction (a noise, a thought, an emotion, a bodily sensation), then gently return the attention to the breath. This process of noting thoughts and sensations, then returning the awareness to the breath is repeated for the duration of the sitting. Though the practice may sound boring, it's remarkable how any experience, including boredom, becomes interesting when it's an object of moment-to-moment investigation.

Little by little, with regular practice, you start to discriminate raw sensory events from your reactions to them. Eventually, you begin to experience a point of stillness within. As the stillness becomes more stable, you tend to identify less with fleeting thoughts and feelings, such as fear, anger, or pain, and experience a state of inner harmony, regardless of changing circumstances. For me, meditation is a tool that allows me to stay calm and centered (well, most of the time) during the stressful highs and lows of basketball and life outside the arena. During games I often get agitated by bad calls, but years of meditation practice have taught me how to find that still point within so that I can argue passionately with the refs without being overwhelmed by anger.

How do the players take to meditation? Some of them find the exercises amusing. Bill Cartwright once quipped that he liked the sessions because they gave him extra time to take a nap. But even those players who drift off during meditation practice get the basic point: *awareness is everything*. Also, the experience of sitting silently together in a group tends to bring about a subtle shift in consciousness that strengthens the team bond. Sometimes we extend mindfulness to the court and conduct whole practices in silence. The deep level of concentration and nonverbal communication that arises when we do this never fails to astonish me.

More than any other player, B. J. Armstrong took meditation to heart and studied it on his own. Indeed, he attributes much of his success as a player to his understanding of *not thinking, just doing*. "A lot of guys second-guess themselves," he says. "They don't know whether to pass or shoot or what. But I just go for it. If I'm open, I'll shoot, and if I'm not, I'll pass. When there's a loose ball, I just go after it. The game happens so fast, the less I can think and the more I can just react to what's going on, the better it will be for me and, ultimately, the team."

VISUALIZATION

As any fan knows, basketball is an incredibly fast-paced, high-energy game. During time-outs the players are often so revved up, they can't concentrate on what I'm saying. To help them cool down mentally as well as physically, I've developed a quickie visualization exercise I call *the safe spot*.

During the fifteen or thirty seconds they have to grab a drink and towel off, I encourage them to picture themselves someplace where they feel secure. It's a way for them to take a short mental vacation before addressing the problem at hand. Simple as it may seem, the exercise helps players reduce their anxiety and focus their attention on what they need to do when they return to the court.

B.J., Scottie and other players also practice visualization before games. "I believe that if I can take twenty or thirty minutes before each game and visualize what's going to happen," says Armstrong, "I'll be able to react to it without thinking, because I'll already have seen it in my mind. When I'm lying down before the game, I can see myself making a shot or boxing out or getting a loose ball. And then when I see that come up during the game, I don't think about it, I do it. There are no second thoughts, no hesitation. Sometimes, after the game, I'll go, 'Wow! I saw that! I anticipated it before it happened.'"

Vizualization is an important tool for me. Coaching requires a free-ranging imagination, but during the heat of the season it's easy to get wound up so tight that you strangle your own creativity. Visualization is the bridge I use to link the grand vision of the team I conjure up every summer to the evolving reality on the court. That vision becomes a working sketch that I adjust, refine and sometimes scrap altogether as the season develops.

One of my strengths as a coach is my ability, developed over years of practice, to visualize ways to short-circuit opponents' offensive schemes. Sometimes if I can't call up a clear image of the other team in my mind, I'll study videotapes for hours until I have a strong cnough "feel" for the opponent to start toying around with ideas. During one of those sessions, I visualized a way to neutralize Magic Johnson: double-teaming him in the back court to force him to give up the ball. That was one of the keys to beating the Lakers to win our first championship in 1991.

Before each game, I usually do forty-five minutes of visualization at home to prepare my mind and come up with last-minute adjustments. This is an outgrowth of the pregame sessions I did when I played with the Knicks. When I started coaching in the CBA, I didn't give myself enough time for this ritual, and I often got so tense during games I'd lash out at the referees and get called repeatedly for technicals. Once I was suspended for bumping up against a ref during an argument. At that point I realized I needed to become more detached emotionally and put the game in the proper perspective.

My pregame sessions are not unlike what my father did during his early morning devotions. I usually call up images of the players in my mind and try to "embrace them in the light," to use the Pentecostal parlance that has been adopted by the New Age. Sometimes an individual player cries out for attention because of an injury or a difficult upcoming matchup. When Horace Grant was matched up against someone like Karl Malone, for instance, I'd focus on what he needed to do. "This is going to be a real test of your manhood, Horace," I'd say before the game. "We'll help you out as much as we can, but you're going to have to be the door that doesn't open." Sometimes a few words was all he needed to raise his game to another level.

INTIMACY WITH ALL THINGS

Another important aspect of what we do is to create a supportive environment for the players where they feel secure and free from constant scrutiny. Although we maintain high standards, we do everything possible to prevent the players from feeling *personally* responsible when the team loses.

When I took over the Bulls in 1989, I told the players that, as far as I was concerned, the only people who really mattered were the team's inner circle: the twelve players, the four coaches, the trainer, and the equipment manager. Everyone else was an outsider, even Jerry Krause. The idea was to heighten the feeling of intimacy, the sense that we were engaged in something sacred and inviolate. To protect the sanctity of the group, I keep the media out of practices and restrict the number of people who travel with the team. I also instruct the players not to blab to the press about everything we do. In order to build trust, the players need to know that they can be open and honest with each other, without seeing their words in the paper the next day.

Part of my motivation is to protect the team, and Michael himself, from the Jordan phenomenon. Everywhere we go, legions of reporters, celebrities, and star-struck fans surround us, trying to get close to Michael. When I was with the Knicks, I had seen what this kind of invasion could do to a team. The Knicks were a hot item in the early seventies and attracted a gaggle of movie stars, politicians, and other high-profile hangers-on. Even though Red Holzman kept the group exclusive, our retinue grew so large that the players eventually lost each other in the crush.

Michael's popularity makes it virtually impossible for the team to do anything together in public, except play the game. So we have to turn our practice sessions into bonding rituals. When I was a player, I used to have a slogan Scotch-taped to the mirror in my apartment: "Make your work play and your play work." Basketball is a form of play, of course, but it's easy for players to lose sight of this because of the pressures of the job. As a result, my primary goal during practice is to get the players to reconnect with the intrinsic joy of the game. Some of our most exhilarating moments as a team come at these times. That's certainly true for Jordan, who loves practice, especially the scrimmages, because it's pure basketball, nothing extra.

Not everything I've tried in practice works, however. At one session, I had the players do an exercise suggested by a prominent Chicago psychiatrist who said it had worked wonders with his patients in releasing pent-up aggression. Obviously, none of his patients were professional basketball players. The basic idea was to assume a crouching gorilla pose and lock eyes with your partner, then jump up and down together, grunting like apes. When we did this exercise in practice, the players literally fell on the floor laughing. It reminded them of the chest thumping and ape-like posturing of the New York Knicks. Needless to say, I never tried that one again.

ENGAGING THE MIND, HARNESSING THE SPIRIT

It's easy for players to get so caught up in the fantasy world of the NBA that they lose touch with reality. My job, as I see it, is to wake them out of that dreamlike state and get them grounded in the real world. That's why I like to introduce them to ideas outside the realm of the game, to show them that there's more to life than basketball—and *more to basketball than basketball.*

Challenging the players' minds and getting them to share their views on topics other than basketball helps build solidarity, too. Some coaches try to force players to bond with each other by putting them through hellish Marine Corps–style training. That's a short-term solution, at best. I've found that the connection will be deeper and last longer if it's built on a foundation of genuine exchange.

One way we do that is to talk regularly about ethics. Every season, after we've narrowed the team down to the basic twelve-man roster, I pass out a handbook that's a modern-day reinterpretation of the Ten Commandments. During practices one of the players will read a section from the book to stimulate group discussion. Once we had a heated debate about guns after I noticed someone carrying a weapon on the team plane. Guns were becoming a fad in the NBA, and some of the players insisted they needed them for protection. I had a different point of view. When I was with the Knicks, I once got into an argument with a ref that made me screaming mad. Finally, after I finished my tirade, the Knicks' trainer, Danny Whelan said, "So, if you had a gun you'd shoot him, right?" That stopped me cold. He was right. I was so angry I could have easily thrown a punch at the ref, so what was going to stop me from pulling a gun out if I had one handy? The Bulls needed to learn that before something tragic happened.

Another way I expand the players' minds is by giving them books to read on road trips. Titles I've handed out include: *Fever: Twelve Stories* by John Wideman (for Michael Jordan), *Ways of the White Folks* by Langston Hughes (Scottie Pippen), *On the Road* by Jack Kerouac (Will Perdue), *All the Pretty Horses* by Cormac McCarthy (Steve Kerr), and *Beavis & Butt-Head: This Book Sucks* by Mike Judge (Stacey King). In some cases, I've selected books that explore spiritual issues. B. J. Armstrong has read *Zen Mind, Beginner's Mind*, while John Paxson bravely struggled through *Zen and the Art of Motorcycle Maintenance*. Horace Grant became an avid reader after devouring *Joshua: A Parable for Today* by Joseph F. Grizone, and Craig Hodges was inspired by *Way of the Peaceful Warrior*, Dan Millman's book about an athlete who turns inward to rediscover his competitive spirit.

Jerry Krause places a premium on finding players with "good character," and that usually means they have a strong religious background of some kind. Hodges is a good example. When asked to describe himself in three words or less on a pr department questionnaire, he wrote, "searching for truth." What I liked about Craig was his selfless approach to the game. A devoted student of Islam, he felt the Bulls were on a sacred mission, and he was willing to do anything to further the quest. During my first year as head coach, he was hobbled by a foot injury and lost his starting job to John Paxson. Someone else in that position might have spent the whole season bellyaching about his predicament. Not

Craig. "I could have gone on an ego trip, but I didn't," he says, "because I knew we were in the midst of something really great."

PUTTING IT TOGETHER

In 1990 the team finally started to click. At first some of the players were skeptical about the triangle offense. B. J. Armstrong, for one, couldn't believe that it was the answer to every defense imaginable, as Tex Winter claimed. But when we started winning consistently, the players changed their tune. What they liked most about the system was that it was democratic: it created shots for everyone, not just the superstars. "The system gives us direction, keeps us all on the same page," B. J. said. "If you're just running plays for individuals, that separates you from one another. If it's play X, you know who's going to shoot all the time, and pretty soon you're like a dog that's getting hit—you don't want to do it because there's no incentive for you. But in the system *anyone* can shoot, *anyone* can score, *anyone* can make the pass. The system responds to whoever is open."

It didn't always work that way in the beginning, however. Sometimes it looked like the players were on five different pages in five different books. But the players were working in harmony with each other, and that meant a lot. The team started coming together in the second half of the 1989–90 season and had the second best record in the league after the All-Star break. We cruised through the first two rounds of the playoffs, beating the Milwaukee Bucks, 3–1, and the Philadelphia 76ers, 4–1.

Detroit was another story. We'd only beaten the Pistons once during the regular season that year, but we still had high expectations for the series. Unfortunately, we didn't have the home court advantage, which turned out to be the difference. Though the triangle offense helped open up shots, most of the players were still intimidated by Detroit's defense. They got nervous as the pressure mounted, and relied too heavily on Jordan when the 24-second clock was running down. And the Pistons descended upon Jordan in threes, knocking him to the floor several times in the first game.

In Game 2, Jordan, nursing a sore hip and a bruised wrist, scored only 7 points in the first half. At half time he stormed into the locker room and kicked over a chair, furious at his teammates for not picking up the slack. I followed him into the room and echoed the theme, telling the players I thought they were playing tentative, scared basketball. They weren't attacking the hoop or taking good shots; they were just throwing the ball up, praying for it to go in. That explosion woke them up. Even though they still lost the game, they played much more courageously in the series from that point on.

The finale was Game 7 in Detroit. Winning the seventh game of a playoff series on the road is difficult no matter what the circumstances, but we had two additional obstacles. John Paxson was out with a sprained ankle, and Scottie Pippen had a migraine headache. The result was an embarrassing 93–74 loss, our weakest performance all season.

This was the Bulls' crisis point. Losing that game in such a humiliating way sealed the team's bond. After the game, Jerry Krause, who rarely gets emotional in front of the team, burst into the locker room and started venting his frustration. As he left, he slammed the door behind him and vowed this kind of defeat would never happen again.

Truth be told, Jerry didn't have to say a word. Everyone in the room knew exactly what needed to be done. They'd gotten so close to victory they could smell it.

Early the next day, assistant coach Jim Cleamons dropped by our training center in Deerfield to do some paperwork. Over in the corner of the weight room, he could see Horace Grant and Scottie Pippen working out with weights.

They were already preparing for the next season.

chapter EIGHT

AGGRESSIVENESS

WITHOUT ANGER

*Fundamentally, the marksman aims at
himself.*

—EUGEN HERRIGEL

That summer in Montana, I realized that anger was the Bulls' real enemy, not the Detroit Pistons. Anger was the restless demon that seized the group mind and kept the players from being fully awake. Whenever we went to Detroit, the unity and awareness we'd worked so hard to build collapsed, and the players reverted to their most primitive instincts.

That response was disappointing, but hardly surprising. It was how they'd originally been trained to play the game. Win or die was the code; rousing the players' anger and bloodlust was the method. But that kind of approach, though it often gets the players' juices flowing, interferes with concentration and ultimately backfires.

It also stinks as a blueprint for competition.

St. Augustine said, "Anger is a weed; hate is the tree." Anger only breeds more anger and eventually fuels violence—on the streets or in professional sports.

A JAB FOR A JAB

It was no coincidence that the players had a hard time staying focused against Detroit. The Pistons' primary objective was to throw us off our game by raising the level of violence on the floor. They pounded away at the players ruthlessly, pushing, shoving, sometimes even headbutting, to provoke them into retaliating. As soon as that happened, the battle was over.

The Bulls had a long, ugly history of battling the Pistons. In 1988 a brawl erupted during a game when Detroit's Rick Mahorn, a 6'10", 260-pound bruiser, fouled Jordan hard on his way to the hoop. Head coach Doug Collins, who weighed in at 195 pounds, tried to quell the disturbance by jumping on Mahorn's back and attempting to wrestle him to the floor. But Mahorn spun around and sent Collins crashing into the scorers' table. During another game in 1989, Isiah Thomas slugged Bill Cartwright in the head after running into one of Bill's elbows. Cartwright, who had never been punched before in a game, hit back, and both players were fined and suspended. Isiah fractured his left hand and missed a good part of the season.

Scottie Pippen had the most punishing assignment of all. On defense, he had to cover Hatchet Man No. 1, Bill Laimbeer, and on offense, he matched up against Hatchet Man No. 2, Dennis

Rodman. Pippen got into some royal battles with Laimbeer, who was four inches taller and outweighed him by at least forty-five pounds. In the 1989 playoffs, Laimbeer elbowed Scottie in the head and gave him a concussion during a tussle over a rebound. The following year, in Game 5 of the playoffs, Scottie took Laimbeer down with a necktie tackle as he was driving to the basket. Afterwards, according to Jordan, Laimbeer threatened to break Michael's neck in retaliation.

I wasn't happy with what Scottie had done. It was foolhardy and dangerous. But I understood only too well the line between playing hard and playing angry. When I played for the Knicks, I had a reputation for being a tough defender and opponents consistently read malevolence into the aggressive way I used my elbows. It was during the 1971–72 playoffs that I learned once and for all that mean-spirited aggression is never worth the price.

The man who taught me that lesson was Jack Marin, a tough, no-nonsense forward for the Baltimore Bullets who liked to bait Bill Bradley, calling him a "pinko liberal" to rattle him. Marin was an emotional time bomb, and I knew if I could get him angry enough, he would do something stupid. So before a key game I devised a scheme to provoke him that I feel embarrassed about to this day. Late in the fourth quarter, I gave him a little shove as he dribbled toward the basket. Then I confronted him at midcourt and shoved him again. That did it. He whipped around and threw a punch. The next thing he knew, he was ejected—it was his sixth foul—and we went on to win the game.

Marin held on to his anger until the next time we faced each other, almost a year later. All of a sudden, as I was going for the hoop, he took a shot at me and I went crashing to the floor. It was a painful lesson, but what Marin showed me was that using anger to defeat an opponent inevitably comes back to haunt you.

A   B R I E F   H I S T O R Y   O F   N B A
W A R F A R E

In those days, brawling was a common occurrence in the NBA. Most teams had an enforcer—the Celtics' "Jungle Jim" Loscutoff was the prototype—whose primary job was to protect his teammates when the going got rough. The Knicks' enforcer during my first two years was Walt Bellamy, a 6'10½", 245-pound center, but he was missing in action when I had my baptism by fire. The game was against the Hawks, who had just moved to Atlanta from St. Louis and were playing temporarily in a stadium at Georgia Tech, where there was no soundproofing in the locker rooms. Before the game we could hear the Hawks' coach, Richie Guerin, inciting his players to wage war against us. Guerin wasn't my biggest fan. The year before I had cut open forward Bill Bridges' forehead with my elbow, and Guerin was so enraged he ordered another player, Paul Silas, to pay me back. Silas didn't get around to it in that game, but he hadn't forgotten Guerin's charge.

With about thirty seconds left in the first half, I got the ball near the basket and started making a move on Silas when he shoved me in the back and sent me sprawling across the floor. As I got up and handed the ball to the ref, Silas took a wayward swing at my head. I dodged the blow and walked to the free-throw line, trying, as best I could, to stay calm.

At halftime the tirade in the other locker room continued, and tensions escalated. Finally, late in the game, a brawl erupted when one of the Atlanta players threw a punch at Willis Reed. Ironically, the only player on either team who didn't participate in the fight was Bellamy, who had withdrawn psychically from the team because of a dispute with management.

Soon after that game, the NBA started taking steps to reduce violence on court. First, players were fined, and, in some cases, suspended, for coming off the bench and joining in a brawl. Next, the league clamped down on throwing punches: anyone who struck another player was immediately ejected and suspended for at least one game. Those changes didn't eliminate violence; they merely gave it a different face. Hall of Fame enforcer Wes Unseld argued that the no-punching rule gave the bullies in the league license to hammer away at players and get away with all kinds of treachery without having to worry about retribution. In the late 1980s, the era of the Detroit Bad Boys, the NBA instituted a new rule severely penalizing players for committing "flagrant" fouls, malicious acts away from the ball that could cause serious injury. That helped, but some teams, in particular, the New York Knicks, still found ways to intimidate their opponents with brute force. So the league changed the rules again in 1994–95, restricting hand-checking and double-teaming in certain situations.

But the problem of uncontrolled anger and brutality rages on. Writer Kevin Simpson offered this analysis in *The Sporting News*. "It's not so much that violence in the NBA has flown out of control, but that deliberate violence has become the next step in a progression of sports culture. While the league has reveled in the raw, physical prowess of its athletes and promoted the game accordingly, it has also presided—unwittingly—over a kind of spiritual deterioration, one that has seen an attitude of intimidation become the preeminent force on the floor."

FURTHER ALONG THE PATH OF
THE WARRIOR

There *has* to be another way, an approach that honors the humanity of both sides while recognizing that only one victor can
emerge. A blueprint for giving your all out of respect for the
battle, never hatred of the enemy. And, most of all, a wide-angle
view of competition that encompasses both opponents as partners
in the dance.

Black Elk spoke of directing love and generosity of spirit
toward the white man, even as his people's land was being taken
away. And in *Shambhala: The Sacred Path of the Warrior*, Tibetan
Buddhist teacher Chogyam Trungpa wrote, "The challenge of
warriorship is to step out of the cocoon, to step out into space,
by being brave and at the same time gentle."

This is the attitude I try to encourage. It's a direct extension
of the Lakota ideal of teamwork we started experimenting with
during my years as an assistant coach. In the beginning, though
the players were interested, it wasn't easy to turn their minds
around. They'd been conditioned since early adolescence to think
that every confrontation was a personal test of manhood. Their
first instinct was to use force to solve every problem. What I
tried to do was get them to walk away from confrontations and
not let themselves be distracted. If somebody fouled them hard,
I suggested turning around, taking a deep breath, and staying as
composed as possible so they could keep their minds fixed on
the goal: victory.

The system reinforces this perspective. The strength of the
triangle offense is that it's based on the Taoist principle of yielding
to an opponent's force in order to render him powerless. The

idea is not to wilt or act dishonorably in the face of overwhelming force, but to be savvy enough to use the enemy's own power against him. If you look hard enough, you'll find his weaknesses. Bottom line: there's no need to overpower when you can outsmart.

For the strategy to work, all five players have to be moving in sync so that they can take advantage of the openings that occur when the defense overextends itself. If one player gets caught in a tussle with his man, resisting the pressure rather than moving away from it, he can jam up the whole system. That lesson has to be constantly reinforced. Once in a game against the Miami Heat in 1991, I called a timeout when I saw Scottie Pippen get into a trash-talking war with the other side. Scottie knew what I was going to say, and got defensive as soon as I started talking. But Cliff Levingston, a cheerful, fun-loving forward whose nickname was Good News, defused the tension, saying, "Come on, Pip. You know Phil's right." Afterwards, we talked about the incident, as an example of how we had to grow as a team and not retaliate every time our opponents did something we didn't like.

Teaching the players to embrace a nonbelligerent way of thinking about competition required continuous reinforcement. One of the first steps I took was to institute a series of "silly" fines to discourage players from insulting the other team. Example: a big man will get fined $10 for taking three-point shots at the end of the game when we're ahead by 20 or more points. That kind of shot demeans your opponent and only builds rage that might be returned later on.

I also discourage players from turning a good move into a humiliating one. Example: in the 1994 playoffs against the Knicks, Scottie Pippen drove to the basket and sent Patrick Ewing sprawling to the floor. After dunking the ball, Scottie straddled Ewing and waved his finger in Ewing's face. What did that accomplish? Pippen got a little ego rush, but he also got called for a technical and planted a seed of anger in the Knicks', not to mention the refs', minds.

Sometimes I use our opponents' anger to try to motivate the team. There's a clip from a Bulls-Knicks game I often screen that shows Ewing pounding his chest and yelling, "Fuck those motherfuckers!" That feeling is what the players have to steel themselves against. They have to develop a certain grittiness and dogged determination to stand up to brutality without being lured into the fray.

EXTENDING THE METAPHOR

The implications of using the warrior ideal as a way of redirecting aggressive energy reach far beyond the NBA. The need is painfully obvious. A couple of years ago I watched a New York City high school championship game in Madison Square Garden that made my heart sink. It was a messy game, marred by a lot of in-your-face posturing and dirty tactics. When it was over, the winning team approached the losers and started taunting them until a fight broke out. That kind of confrontation, which often leads to tragic consequences, wouldn't be so prevalent if young people knew how to preserve their pride and dignity without blindly acting out their anger.

There are those who've already picked up the ball. Ellen Riley, one of the few women who attended the Beyond Basketball workshop at the Omega Institute, is using the warrior model in an educational training program for at-risk teenagers in Yonkers,

New York. Although it's not a sports program, the students have embraced the warrior imagery and the ideals of dedication and commitment. "What we're trying to convey is that individual performance is important, but it has to be embedded in a much larger context," Riley explains. "Being a responsible member of a community, or team, is simply the most effective way to live."

TESTING THE WATERS

My goal in 1990–91 was to win the conference title and the home-court advantage in the playoffs. We had proved that we could beat the Pistons at home, but we didn't have the poise yet to win consistently in their arena. Until that happened, we needed to capture the conference title so that we could benefit from the unnerving effect Chicago Stadium, the loudest arena in the NBA, had on visiting teams. That year we won 26 straight games at home, the longest streak in the history of the franchise. I cautioned the players not to get too excited about victories or too depressed about defeats. When we lost, I'd say, "Okay, let's flush that one down the drain when you shower. Let's not lose two in a row." That became our motto for the season, and after mid-December we lost two straight only once. I also warned the team about becoming complacent with a three-game winning streak. If they let the momentum build, they could extend a streak to eight, nine, ten games. Winning started to come naturally. Going into a tough road trip, I'd say it would be great if we won five of the next seven games. Michael would reply confidently, "We'll win 'em all."

The first big test came on February 7 in a game against the Pistons at the Palace in Auburn Hills, Michigan. We hadn't won a game in the Palace since Game 1 of the 1989 playoffs, but this time Isiah Thomas would be out of action with a wrist injury.

Studying Detroit game films that week, I uncovered a clue to the Palace mystique: the rim of the basket closest to the Pistons' bench was stiffer than the one on the other end. This meant that off-line shots would be less likely to get a good bounce and go in. We had rarely shot well at that basket, and I had always chalked it up to the players' lack of poise in front of the Detroit bench. But perhaps a subtle act of gamesmanship was also a contributing factor. (Adjusting the rigidity of the baskets is not uncommon in the NBA. Some teams also install fast nets to speed up the tempo of a game or deflate the balls to slow it down.) As the visiting coach, I got to pick which basket we would shoot at in the first half. I usually chose the basket in front of our bench, so we would be playing defense at our end of the court in the second half. But this time I reversed strategy: the last thing I wanted was to have the players shooting at a rigged basket in the closing minutes of the game.

More important to me, however, was how the players dealt with Detroit's intimidation tactics, and I began to see some promising signs. Even though Bill Cartwright was ejected in the first half for elbowing Bill Laimbeer (okay, so the gentle warrior image was not in evidence every second of every game), the team didn't collapse when Cartwright left the floor. The younger players, especially Scottie and Horace, managed to maintain their focus. At one point somebody knocked Horace's goggles off and I thought he might unravel. But he recovered gracefully and raced back on defense after assistant coach Jim Cleamons jumped up and screamed, "Just play through it!" B. J. Armstrong also seemed unfazed by the Bad Boys' ploys and scored clutch baskets in the fourth quarter, as the team held on to win, 95–93. After the game, Jordan announced triumphantly to the media, "A monkey is off our back."

That's when the team really started to gel. We went 11–1 in February, the Bull's most successful month ever, and began to put long winning streaks together. Around this time Bill Cartwright and John Paxson decided to give up alcohol for Lent. They did it, in part, to set an example for the young players, to show that they were willing to make sacrifices to win a championship. Three or four other players joined in, and they continued to abstain till the end of the season.

RIGHTEOUS ANGER

Not everything went smoothly, however. On April Fool's Day, Stacey King, who had been carping at reporters about not getting enough playing time, walked out of practice. This act of rebellion had been building for months. Stacey, a forward who had been one of the nation's leading scorers in college, was having a difficult time adjusting to his role as a bench player. I had been patient with him, but the selfishness of his remarks pushed me over the edge. I decided to fine him $250 and suspend him for the next game, which would cost him about $12,000 in salary. When he showed up for practice the following day, we got into a shouting match in my office. I lost control and called him a "fat ass" and a few other less flattering names.

I wasn't proud of my performance, but my tirade had a positive effect on Stacey. Before that episode he had a distorted view of his role on the team, and some of the veterans felt he needed a dose of reality therapy to bring him in line. They were right. After sitting out a game and thinking over what he had done, he dropped the attitude. He never gave me a problem again.

As a rule I try not to unleash my anger at players that way. When it happens, I say what I have to say, then let it pass, so the bad feelings won't linger in the air and poison the team. Sometimes what my father called "righteous anger" is the most skillful means to shake up a team. But it has to be dispensed judiciously. And it's got to be genuine. If you're not really angry, the players will detect it immediately.

Most importantly, eruptions shouldn't be directed at one or two members of a group; they should encompass the whole pack. The first time I got visibly angry at the team, after a loss to the Orlando Magic during my first year as head coach, the players were speechless because they had never seen that side of me before. It was right after the All-Star Game, which had taken place in Orlando, and many of the players had been hanging out in Florida all week, chasing women and partying every night. I was angry because we had blown a 17-point lead, and it was clear that the players' extracurricular activities were sapping their energy. After the game I kicked a can of soda across the locker room and gave the players a fire-and-brimstone sermon on dedicating themselves to winning and doing everything possible, on *and* off the court, to become champions. The next day the flock of groupies that had gathered around the team was nowhere in sight.

ONE INSTANT IS ETERNITY

We ended the 1990–91 season on a romp, beating Detroit in the final game, and finished with the best record in the conference:

61–21. Then after beating New York, 3–0, and Philadelphia, 4–1, in the early rounds of the playoffs, we faced Detroit again. The Pistons were hobbling after a tough series against Boston and several of their players, including Isiah Thomas and Joe Dumars, were nursing injuries. But that didn't make them any less arrogant.

This time we didn't *have* to use Michael as much as we had in the past. He didn't have to score 35 to 40 points a game because Scottie Pippen, Horace Grant, and the bench had learned how to take advantage of the openings Michael created by acting as a decoy and drawing the Detroit defense in his direction. In Game 1 he went 6 for 15 and scored only 22 points, but the reserves—Will Perdue, Cliff Levingston, B. J. Armstrong, and Craig Hodges—went on a surge in the fourth quarter and put the team ahead to stay.

As we moved toward a four-game sweep, the Pistons got more and more desperate. Scottie, as usual, took much of the abuse. Forward Mark Aguirre was relentless. "You're dead, Pippen, you're dead," he jabbered, according to an account in *The Jordan Rules*. "I'm getting you in the parking lot after the game. Don't turn your head, because I'm going to kill you. You're fuckin' dead." Scottie just laughed it off. In Game 4, Dennis Rodman shoved Pippen into the stands so hard it took him a few seconds to stagger to his feet. As he got up, Horace rushed over and screamed, "You play, you play!" Scottie shrugged it off and kept playing. "They really weren't focusing on basketball," he told reporters afterwards. "Basically Rodman's been making those stupid plays for the last couple of years, but I've been retaliating and giving him the opportunity to let that work to his advantage. We put our main focus into basketball, as we have all season."

Scottie wasn't alone. Everybody on the team was slammed around. John Paxson was thrown into the stands by Laimbeer. Other players were tackled, tripped, elbowed, and smacked in the face. But they all laughed it off. The Pistons didn't know how to respond. We completely disarmed them by not striking back. At that moment, our players became true champions.

The Pistons, on the other hand, gave up being champions long before the final whistle blew. In the final minutes of Game 4, which we won 115–94, four of Detroit's starters, Thomas, Laimbeer, Rodman, and Aguirre, got up from the bench and walked out of the arena scowling. On their way out, they passed by our bench without even acknowledging our presence.

After that series, the finals against the Los Angeles Lakers were anticlimactic. The Lakers won the first game in Chicago, 93–91, on a late three-pointer by forward Sam Perkins, but that was their last shining moment. After that our defense took over, pressuring Magic Johnson, keeping the ball out of his hands and double-teaming their post-up players, James Worthy and Vlade Divac. We won in five games, taking the last three in L.A.

The emergence of John Paxson as a clutch shooter was another key. When Jordan was pressed, he often dished the ball to Paxson, who shot 65 percent from the field during the series and scored 20 points in the final game, including the shot that sealed the win. After Game 4, Magic summed up the situation beautifully: "It's not just Michael. He's going great, but so is the team. It's one thing if he's going great and the team isn't. Then you have a chance to win. They've got Horace playing well; Bill is playing solid; and their bench is playing outstanding. They've got the total game going."

Before the final game, the Disney organization asked Jordan if he would do one of their "What are you going to do now?"

commercials. He said he'd do it only if the ad included his teammates. This was a sign of how far Michael, and the team, had
come. It brought back memories of the 1973 Knicks. After we
won the title that year, Vaseline wanted Bill Bradley to do a
post-victory commercial, but he suggested the company use his
teammates instead. As it turned out, Donnie May, Bills stand-
in, ended up playing the starring role.

Here I was again at another victory party in L.A. After we
stopped for a moment to say the Lord's Prayer, the champagne
started flowing. It was an emotional scene. Scottie Pippen popped
the first bottle of bubbly and poured it over Horace Grant's head.
Bill Cartwright took a sip of champagne and sighed, "Finally."
Sam Smith reported that B. J. Armstrong, Dennis Hopson, Stacey
King, and Cliff Levingston serenaded Tex Winter with an
impromptu rap song: "Oh, we believe in the triangle, Tex. We
believe, yeah, we believe in that triangle. It's the show for those
in the know." His eyes filled with tears, Michael Jordan hugged
the championship trophy as if it were a newborn baby.

Strangely, I was somewhat detached. This was the players'
show, and I didn't feel the same euphoria they did. But there was
one last point I wanted to make.

Midway through the festivities, I gave my last speech of the
season. "You should know," I said, "that many championship
teams don't come back. This is a business. I'd like to have all of
you back, but it doesn't always happen. But this is something
special you have shared and which you'll never forget. This will
be yours forever and it will always be a bond that will keep you
together. I want to thank you all personally for this season. Now,
get back to the party."

THE INVISIBLE

LEADER

*A good merchant hides his goods and
appears to have nothing; a skilled
craftsman leaves no traces.*

—LAO-TZU

John Paxson once came across a Chinese fable in the *Harvard Business Review* that he said reminded him of my leadership style.

The story was about Emperor Liu Bang, who, in the third century B.C., became the first ruler to consolidate China into a unified empire. To celebrate his victory, Liu Bang held a great banquet in the palace, inviting many important government officials, military leaders, poets, and teachers, including Chen Cen, a master who had given him guidance during the campaign. Chen Cen's disciples, who accompanied him to the banquet, were impressed by the proceedings but were baffled by an enigma at the heart of the celebration.

Seated at the central table with Liu Bang was his illustrious high command. First there was Xiao He, an eminent general whose knowledge of military logistics was second to none. Next to him was Han Xin, a legendary tactitian who'd won every battle he'd ever fought. Last was Chang Yang, a shrewd diplomat who was gifted at convincing heads of state to form alliances and surrender without fighting. These men the disciples could understand. What puzzled them was how Liu Bang, who didn't have a noble birth or knowledge comparable to that of his chief advisers, fit into the picture. "Why is he the emperor?" they asked.

Chen Cen smiled and asked them what determines the strength of a wheel. "Is it not the sturdiness of the spokes?" one responded. "Then why is it that two wheels made of identical spokes differ in strength?" asked Chen Cen. After a moment, he continued, "See beyond what is seen. Never forget that a wheel is made not only of spokes but also of the space between the spokes. Sturdy spokes poorly placed make a weak wheel. Whether their full potential is realized depends on the harmony between. The essence of wheelmaking lies in the craftman's ability to conceive and create the space that holds and balances the spokes within the wheel. Think now, who is the craftsman here?"

The disciples were silent until one of them said, "But master, how does a craftsman secure the harmony between the spokes?" Chen Cen asked them to think of sunlight. "The sun nurtures and vitalizes the trees and flowers," he said. "It does so by giving away its light. But in the end, in which direction do they grow? So it is with a master craftsman like Liu Bang. After placing individuals in positions that fully realize their potential, he secures harmony among them by giving them all credit for their distinctive achievements. And in the end, as the trees and flowers grow toward the giver, the sun, individuals grow toward Liu Bang with devotion."

THE MIDDLE WAY

Many coaches are control-oholics. They keep a tight rein on everyone from the players to the equipment manager, and set strict guidelines for how each person should perform. Everything flows from the top, and the players dare not think for themselves. That approach may work in isolated cases, but it usually only creates resentment, particularly with the NBA's young breed of players, who are more independent than their predecessors. Witness what happened to Don Nelson when he was head coach/ general manager of the Golden State Warriors. He got into a battle of wills with a sensitive star, Chris Webber, that destroyed the team and ultimately forced Nelson to resign.

Other coaches are far more *laissez-faire*. Feeling helpless about controlling their players, who generally make much more money than they do, they give them total freedom, hoping that somehow they'll figure out a way to win on their own. It's a difficult situation: even when coaches want to exercise more control, the league doesn't give them much ammunition with which to discipline players. Fines of $250 a day, the maximum that coaches can mete out, are meaningless to the new generation of multimillionaires. When Butch Beard took over as head coach of the New Jersey Nets in 1994, he instituted a simple dress code for road trips. Free spirit Derrick Coleman objected to the policy and, rather than cooperate, paid fines the whole season. Given this climate, some coaches believe the only sensible solution is to pander to their players' absurd demands. They coddle the top two or three stars, try to keep the next five or six players as happy as possible, and hope that the rest don't start a rebellion. Unless they're incredibly gifted psychologists, these coaches inevitably end up feeling as if they're being held hostage by the players they're supposed to be leading.

Our approach is to follow a middle path. Rather than coddling players or making their lives miserable, we try to create a supportive environment that structures the way they relate to each other and gives them the freedom to realize their potential. I also try to cultivate everybody's leadership abilities, to make the players and coaches feel that they've all got a seat at the table. No leader can create a successful team alone, no matter how gifted he is.

What I've learned as a coach, and parent, is that when people are not awed or overwhelmed by authority, true authority is attained, to paraphrase the *Tao Te Ching*. Every leader has weaknessness and screws up some of the time; an effective leader learns to admit that. In coaching the Bulls I try to stay in touch with the same "beginner's mind" I learned to cultivate in Zen practice. As long as I know I *don't* know, chances are I won't do too much harm.

My shortcomings are painfully obvious to me. I have high expectations and don't hand out praise easily. That places an unrealistic burden on some of the players, particularly the younger ones, making them feel that whatever they do will never be enough. Though most players find me compassionate, I'm not a touchy-feely kind of guy who'll slap a fellow on the back and console him when he doesn't perform. I also can be stubborn and intractable, and sometimes I get caught in conflicts with players that rumble on in the background for months before they get resolved.

THE LESSONS OF COMPASSION

The prevailing myth in sports, and the business world, is that managing from the top down and keeping your charges constantly guessing about their status within the organization is an effective way to stimulate creativity. A friend of mine who works for a large corporation told me about a meeting he attended that showed how pervasive this style of management is. His company had been losing some of its best performers to the competition, and top management was perplexed about how to keep the remaining workers happy. A young female executive who had recently been promoted to a senior-level position suggested being more nurturing and compassionate to the worker bees, to encourage them to be more productive. She was roundly attacked by almost everyone at the table. The solution, as top management saw it, was to hire a bunch of "superstars" from outside and give everybody else the message that if they didn't improve dramatically, they would soon be history. Shortly after the meeting, the boss instituted that policy, and, not surprisingly, productivity declined even further.

In his book, *Leading Change*, management consultant James O'Toole talks about a different style of leadership, known as "value-based" management, that closely resembles my approach. "Value-based" leaders, O'Toole says, enlist the hearts and minds of their followers through inclusion and participation. They listen carefully to their followers out of a deep respect for them as individuals and develop a vision that they will embrace because it is based on their highest aspirations. "To be effective," writes O'Toole, "leaders must begin by setting aside that culturally conditioned 'natural' instinct to lead by push, particularly when times are tough. Leaders must instead adopt the unnatural behavior of *always* leading by the pull of inspiring values."

What O'Toole is talking about essentially is compassionate leadership. In the Buddhist tradition, compassion flows from an understanding that everything derives its essential nature, or Buddha nature, from its dependence on everything else. As Pema Chodron, an American Buddhist nun, puts it in her insightful book, *Start Where You Are*: "By being kind to others—if it's done properly, with proper understanding—we benefit as well. So the first point is that we are completely interrelated. What you do to others, you do to yourself. What you do to yourself, you do to others."

In terms of leadership, this means treating everyone with the same care and respect you give yourself—and trying to understand their reality without judgment. When we can do that, we begin to see that we all share basic human struggles, desires, and dreams. With awareness, the barriers between people gently give way, and we begin to understand, directly, remarkably, that we're part of something larger than ourselves.

Horace Grant taught me this lesson. When I became head coach, Horace was still making a lot of mistakes, and I decided to do something drastic to shake him up. I asked him if he minded being criticized in front of the group, and he said no. So I rode him hard in practice—thinking that my words would not only motivate Horace, but also galvanize the other players. If I was particularly harsh in my criticism, the rest of the team would rally around to give him support.

As Horace matured, he asked me to stop treating him that way, and I respected his wish. Then in 1994 a conflict erupted between us when he decided to play out the option on his contract. Early on, Horace had asked my advice on whether he should declare himself a free agent. I told him that if he could live with the risks, he would probably do extremely well financially. But if he went ahead with it, I would expect him to play just as hard in his option year as John Paxson had done a few years earlier. Once the 1993–94 season began, however, I could sense that Horace was pulling away from the team.

During the All-Star Game, he had a flare-up of tendinitis and asked to sit out the next several games. At the time, we were also missing Kukoc, Paxson, and Cartwright, and our lock on first place was in jeopardy. After a few games I told Horace we needed to reactivate him, but he balked, saying, "Coach, I've got to think about next year."

That was the wrong answer. As far as I was concerned, he was getting paid to play *this* year, not next year. The fact that he was going to be a free agent was no excuse. Many of his teammates were in the same situation, but they hadn't retreated from the team.

My anger made me shut down and freeze Horace out of the group. I told him in front of the team that he wasn't living up to the code the Bulls had always honored: play hard, play fair, play *now*. And when he walked out in the middle of practice complaining of tendinitis, I started yelling at him in the trainers' room: "Go home. I don't want to see you around here until you get it together." There were a few expletives mixed in there, as well.

This confrontation troubled me. Why had I been so hard-hearted with Horace? Why did I take his rebellion as a personal affront? Talking it over with my wife, I realized that my own agenda for Horace was getting in the way of seeing the situation clearly. When I stepped back, I saw how much I blamed Horace for trying to sabotage the season when all he was doing was looking out for his future. What I needed to do was open my heart and try to understand the situation from his point of view. I needed to practice the same selflessness and compassion with Horace that I expected from him on court. When I was able to relax the steel grip on my heart and finally see him through a less self-centered lens, our relationship was repaired.

THE DARK SIDE OF SUCCESS

One thing I needed to be particularly mindful of was the effect success was having on the players. Success tends to distort reality and make everybody, coaches as well as players, forget their shortcomings and exaggerate their contributions. Soon they begin to lose sight of what made them successful in the first place: their connection with each other as a team. As Michael Jordan puts it, "Success turns we's back into me's."

I had seen that happen with the New York Knicks after the 1970 championship, and I desperately wanted to protect the Bulls from the same fate. It wasn't easy. After we won our first championship, success nearly tore the team apart. Everybody wanted to take credit for the victory, and several players began clamoring for a bigger role. Scott Williams wanted to shoot more; B. J. Armstrong wanted to be a starter; Horace Grant wanted to be more than just a "blue-collar worker." All of a sudden, I had to spend a lot of time babysitting fragile egos.

I also had to fend off the media invasion. After we won

the championship in 1991, the media presence grew and started feeding off the team. Players who didn't have Jordan's gift for handling reporters were given a national soapbox, and the results were sometimes unfortunate. The first incident occurred before the next season even started. We were invited to a post-championship celebration at the White House in October. Jordan decided not to attend because he had met President Bush before and felt that, if he went, he would be the center of attention. Horace thought it was unfair that Michael was the only player allowed to skip the event and told reporters so. Jordan, he added, "is going to be the death of this team."

Michael wasn't pleased with these remarks, particularly since he had been spending more time with Horace, trying to strengthen their relationship. My guess was that Horace had been manipulated by reporters into speaking out against Jordan. Horace considered it a badge of honor to be honest and forthright, and sometimes he got lured into making pronouncements that sounded a lot more inflammatory than he intended. Jordan seemed to understand this about Horace and didn't take him to task for his remarks.

I could empathize with Horace and other players who got caught in that trap because it had happened to me when I was with the Knicks. Reporters are seductive—that's their job—and if you're inexperienced, they can often trick you into saying something provocative that you'll regret the next day. As a player, I had made some off-the-wall comments to get a laugh or, on occasion, to make a reporter I didn't particularly like stop pestering me. Sometimes I went too far. In 1977 All-Star forward George McGinnis and I got into a tussle, and he leveled what could have been a knockout punch at me from behind. Luckily, I stepped out of the way and the blow merely grazed the side of my head, but I was furious at the refs for not throwing him out of the game. A month or so later when Kermit Washington hit Rudy Tomjanovich in the face and put him out of action for the rest of the season, I was still angry, and made a flip remark to reporters about how it took a black player to hit a white *star* for the league to do something about the violence issue. Out of context, my remarks sounded racist, and insensitive to Tomjanovich, who had sustained massive head injuries. From that point on, I was more circumspect about what I said to the press.

Some coaches try to force players to be close-mouthed by humiliating them in front of their teammates. Former Knicks coach Hubie Brown used to read newspaper stories to his team, sometimes extending practice by a half an hour or more to get through his pile of clips. When Bill Fitch was coaching the Houston Rockets, he used to have the *players* give the readings. Once he had 7'4" center Ralph Sampson, who had made some divisive remarks, stand on a stool in practice and read his quotes aloud to the team.

In my view, that approach only increases the media's power in the players' minds. Instead I try to play the stories down. Once the season starts, I don't pay much attention to the news unless a problem crops up that I have to address. Whenever a "big" story develops, I try to laugh it off in front of the players to show them that I don't consider what appears in the papers to be very important.

When you're young and in the public eye, it's easy to get caught up in fame's seductive web. But the truth is the players aren't fighting for the media or the public, they're fighting for the inner circle of the team. Anyone outside that circle who can destroy the team harmony has to be handled with care.

I'm not always perfectly detached. Sometimes I'll step in if

I think a player is trying to manipulate the media for selfish reasons. At one point, Will Perdue, whose wry wit has made him a media darling, started making noise in the papers about getting more playing time. When I asked him why he had gone public, he said he thought he'd try it because it had worked for Stacey King. I reminded him that Stacey's experiment backfired in the end, costing him a lot of money *and* playing time.

The players have learned a lot about fame watching how Michael Jordan is treated by the press. Writers usually portray him as a larger-than-life superhero or a tarnished celebrity with dark hidden flaws—neither of which is true. That helps the players see through the media's game and become less vulnerable to criticism. Talking about the Bulls' championship run, B. J. Armstrong recalls, "We didn't care about anything they said in the press. That's what kept us together. If a guy said something bad to the press, we didn't care because he was one of our group. That's what enabled us to win three championships in a row."

Over the years the Bulls have been caught up in a number of controversies, such as the White House flap, Pippen and Grant's contract disputes and Jordan's gambling adventures. But none of those well-publicized problems shook the unity of the group. Even when credible rumors that Scottie was going to be traded hovered over the team for the first half of the 1994-95 season, the effect on team play was minimal. Once the game starts, the players know how to tune out those distractions because of the trust they have in each other. The untold story of the Bulls, says B.J. Armstrong, is "the respect each individual has for everybody else."

ALCHEMY

When everything is running smoothly, I, like Lao-tzu's craftsman, try to leave few traces. In the first half of the 1991–92 season, the Bulls were in such perfect harmony they rarely lost. During that period, according to B.J., it felt as if the team was "in tune with nature" and that everything fell into place "like fall and winter and spring and summer."

The team went 36–3 during that stretch. At one point Jerry Reinsdorf asked me if I was driving the team toward the record, and I said no. In truth, it was out of my hands. The Bulls were too good that year to try to slow them down. The only thing that threw them off track briefly was when Michael was ejected from a game, then suspended from another for protesting the call and bumping the ref. We lost both games, and racked up our longest losing streak of the season: two.

This is what I'd been striving for ever since I had started coaching: to become an "invisible" leader. University of Indiana coach Bobby Knight once said that he could never work in the NBA because the coaches don't have any control over the players. My question is: How much control do you need? It's true that NBA coaches don't have the autocratic power of someone like Knight, but we have far more power than it appears. The source of that power is the fact that coaches have played a central role in the players' lives since they were kids. The players are used to having an authority figure telling them what to do, and the only reason they've made it as far as they have is that at some point they listened to what some coach somewhere had to say. The way to tap into that energy is not by being autocratic, but by working *with* the players and giving them increasing responsibility to shape their roles.

SPOKES IN A WHEEL

That's why I like to have strong people around me. When I took over as head coach, I named Tex Winter offensive coordinator and Johnny Bach defensive coordinator. In truth, those distinctions were somewhat artificial; the lines of authority on basketball teams are never that clear cut. But I wanted to make it clear to the players that Tex and Johnny's views should be taken seriously. Tex, Johnny, and I didn't always see things the same way, but the interplay of ideas stimulated everybody's creativity.

The players have also taken on key leadership roles. Scottie Pippen is a good floor leader, energizing the team and inspiring the players to stay focused. B. J. Armstrong provided behind-the-scenes support for the young players; John Paxson was a much-needed voice of reason in the locker room; and Cliff Levingston had an uncanny knack for smoothing over conflicts.

During the championship years, the most important leaders were Bill Cartwright and Michael Jordan. I relied on them to solve minor problems and give me an accurate reading of what was going on with the team. Once during the 1992–93 season, the team went into a slump, losing four out of five games, our worst slide in two years. The next game was against the Utah Jazz, always a tough opponent. On the plane to Salt Lake City, I asked Bill and Michael what they thought we could do to revive the team. They said that some of the players had split themselves off from the group, and I should do something to bring them back together. Bill and Michael were especially concerned about Scottie and Horace, who had recently cooled toward one another after being close friends for so many years.

It was Super Bowl Sunday. When we arrived at the hotel, I told the players to get some pizzas and beers after practice and watch the Super Bowl in their hotel rooms. "You guys need to get together and remember what you're doing this for," I said. "You're *not* doing it for money. It may seem that way, but that's just an external reward. You're doing it for the internal rewards. You're doing it for each other and the love of the game." Michael had a lively Super Bowl party in his room that afternoon, and the players reconnected. The next day they came alive, erasing a 17-point deficit in the fourth quarter to beat Utah 96–92. After that, they settled down and cruised through the rest of the season.

SKILLFUL MEANS

In Buddhist teachings the term *skillful means* is used to describe an approach to making decisions and dealing with problems in a way that is appropriate to the situation and causes no harm. Skillful means always arise out of compassion, and when a problem emerges, the idea is to address the offense without denying the humanity of the offender. A parent who packs a kid off to bed for spilling milk instead of handing the child a sponge is not practicing skillful means.

Like large families, basketball teams are highly charged, com-petitive groups. Because you win or lose as a *team*, individual recognition sometimes gets lost in the larger effort. The result is heightened sensitivity. Everybody is competing with everybody else all the time, and alliances are sometimes tentative and uneasy—a fact of pro sports life that works against deepening intimacy. Players are always complaining about not getting their fair share of playing time or having their role on the team diminished.

Though some coaches try to settle differences in team meetings, I prefer to deal with them on an individual basis. This helps strengthen my one-on-one connection with the players, who sometimes get neglected because we spend so much of our time together *en masse*. Meeting with players privately helps me stay in touch with who they are out of uniform. During the 1995 playoffs, for instance, Toni Kukoc was troubled by reports that Split, Croatia, where his parents live, had been hit by a barrage of artillery fire. It took several days for him to get through on the phone and learn that his family was all right. The war in his homeland is a painful reality of Toni's life. If I ignored that, I probably wouldn't be able to relate to him on any but the most superficial level.

Athletes are not the most verbal breed. That's why bare attention and listening without judgment are so important. When you're a leader, you have to be able to read accurately the subtle messages players send out. To do that means being fully present with beginner's mind. Over the years I've learned to listen closely to players—not just to what they say, but also to their body language and the silence between the words.

I find it amusing when people ask me where I get my ideas for motivating players. The answer is: *in the moment*. My approach to problem-solving is the same as my approach to the game. When a problem arises, I try to read the situation as accurately as possible and respond spontaneously to whatever's happening. I rarely try to apply someone else's ideas to the problem—something I've read in a book, for instance—because that would keep me from tuning in and discovering a fresh, original solution, the most skillful means.

During the 1991 playoffs, Philadelphia's Armon Gilliam was doing a dance on our front line. Scottie was too small to guard him, and Horace had trouble containing him. So, in an inspired moment, I decided to throw Scott Williams, then an untested rookie, at Gilliam, and it worked. To keep Scott from losing his composure in the closing minutes of the game, I told Jordan to keep his eye on him. From then on, Scott, who like Michael is a North Carolina alum, became Jordan's personal project. All because I refused to play the game by the book.

Ultimately, leadership takes a lot of what St. Paul called faith: "the substance of things hoped for, the evidence of things not seen" (Hebrews 11:1). You have to trust your inner knowing. If you have a clear mind and an open heart, you won't have to search for direction. Direction will come to you.

FIVE FINGERS ON A HAND

The Bulls certainly had faith in themselves in 1991–92. At one point, Johnny Bach proclaimed, "Only the Bulls can beat the Bulls," and he was right. Except for a few minor flareups, everything flowed smoothly. There were no serious injuries and only one change in the roster: backup shooting guard Dennis Hopson was replaced by Bobby Hansen. After the All-Star break, the team lost only six games, and we finished with the best record in the league: 67–15.

The playoffs were a different story. After breezing past Miami, we ran into our toughest opponent to date: the New York media. Former Knicks coach Pat Riley had a gift for waging psychological warfare in the papers, and I could see early on when he started complaining to reporters that Jordan was getting breaks from the refs, that this was going to be an explosive series. Riley's strategy worked in the beginning. The combination of the Knicks' brutal style of play, questionable officiating, and negative reporting in the press distracted the players enough to disrupt their game. I decided I had to take a more aggressive stance.

The showdown came in Game 4 in New York. We were ahead in the series, 2–1, and the Knicks needed a win desperately. They started shoving with both hands and tackling dribblers without getting called. Horace compared the game to a World Wrestling Federation match, and Michael told me he thought the officiating was so bad it would be impossible to win. I began making a lot of noise on the sidelines and got thrown out of the game in the second half.

There was something about Riley's manner that brought out my irreverent side. The more self-righteous he got, the more flippant I became. At the press conference after the game, which we lost, 93–86, I said, "I think they're probably licking their chops on Fifth Avenue where the NBA offices are. I think they kind of like that it's a 2–2 series. I don't like 'orchestration' . . . it sounds a little too fishy . . . but they control who they send as referees and if it goes to seven, everybody will be really happy. Everybody will get the TV revenues and ratings they want."

Actually it was Riley who was licking his chops. My remarks, for which I was fined $2,500, gave him the perfect opportunity to work the media. "What [Jackson] is doing is insulting us basically," he said the next day. "I was part of six championship teams. I've been to the finals thirteen times. I know what championship demeanor is all about. The fact that he's whining and whimpering about officiating is an insult to how hard our guys are playing and how much our guys want to win. That's what championship teams are about. They've got to take on all comers. They can't whine about it."

The reporters loved that story line: former New York Knick leaves town and turns into kvetch. I hit back with a few zingers, but I realized Riley had staked out the higher ground and anything I said would only fuel the story. This was an important lesson for me. Though I didn't agree with Riley's characterization of me or the team, there was a grain of truth in what he said. We were the champions, and that meant we had to prove ourselves on every level. The best rejoinder to his remark would be to keep quiet and win the series.

That's what we did. Inspired by Jordan in Game 7, the team finally stopped playing New York's slow, rough-and-tumble game and speeded up the action. In the first quarter, Michael set the tone when he chased down Xavier McDaniel, who had been beating up on Scottie Pippen throughout the series, and blocked one of his shots from behind. The message: you're going to have to go through me to win this one. In the second half, our defense rose to another level, and the Knicks became disheartened. The final score was 110–81. Riley was gracious in defeat. He told reporters he felt we had rediscovered our identity in the final game. "They played like they are," he said.

The rest of the playoffs weren't any easier. The Cleveland Cavaliers, another tough team, took the next series to six games, and the Portland Trail Blazers gave us a scare in the finals when they won Game 2 in Chicago. But we were able to take two out of three in Portland and finished them off in Game 6. Our bench, which had been struggling earlier in the playoffs, came through in that game. The starters had run out of energy, and we had fallen behind by 17 points. But in the fourth quarter a reserve unit, led by Bobby Hansen, who scored a key three-pointer, turned the game around and erased the deficit. For me, this was the sweetest victory because *everybody* on the team made a significant contribution.

The celebration lasted all night. This was the first, and only, time we won a championship in Chicago, and the fans didn't want to leave. After the ceremonies in the locker room, the players returned to the court with the trophy and showed it off to the crowd, dancing in a makeshift chorus line on top of the scorers' table. Later that night, June and I watched our kids play a raucous game of pickup in the backyard. We fell asleep to the sound of basketballs bouncing on the blacktop.

The next season I loosened up. Cartwright had sore knees and a bad back, and we were worried he wouldn't make it to the playoffs. Paxson also had knee problems, and Jordan and Pippen had been worn down by playing in the Olympics. I excused them all from part of training camp, and we started off the season at a much slower pace. Our playbook usually contains a page of specific goals for the season. This time I left that page out. Everyone knew what the goal was: to become the first team since the 1960s to win three championships in a row. In large type on the cover of the playbook, I put the word I felt best described the upcoming season: Triumphant.

We staggered through the season, finishing behind New York in the conference with a 57–25 record. But losing the home-court advantage seemed to energize the players. After winning a brutal six-game series against the Knicks, we faced Charles Barkley and the Phoenix Suns in the finals. They pulled out every trick; we even had to contend with Robin Ficker, a guerrilla fan who sat behind our bench and read excerpts from *The Jordan Rules*.

The crucial turn in the series came in the final seconds of Game 6. The Suns were ahead by 4 with less than a minute to go. But Jordan picked off a rebound and drove down court to bring us within 2. Then with 3.9 seconds left, John Paxson put in a 3-pointer that won the game. I'll never forget what he said afterwards: "You know, it's just like when you're a kid. You go out to your driveway and start counting down 'Three, two, one . . .' I don't know how many shots like that I've taken in my lifetime, but this was the one that really counted."

In my mind, what was impressive about that shot was the pass from Horace Grant that set it up. Horace got the ball from Pippen near the basket and could have tried to muscle his way in for a dunk. But instead he read the court and found Paxson wide open on the periphery. It was a completely unselfish act. This was the player who, four years earlier, Michael Jordan thought would never be able to learn the triangle offense. But when the game was on the line, he did the right thing. Without hesitating he made a selfless play instead of trying to be a hero.

In that split-second all the pieces came together and my role as leader was just as it should be: invisible.

chapter TEN

COACHING

MICHELANGELO

The pauses between the notes—ah,
that is where the art resides!
                    —ARTUR SCHNABEL

When I started working for the Bulls, nobody was more excited than my son, Ben. He worshipped Michael Jordan. He had a huge Jordan poster in his room, read anything he could find about him and talked about him endlessly at the dinner table. Ben's dream was to meet his hero in the flesh.

I mentioned this to Michael my first day on the job, and he made himself available to meet Ben, who was nine at the time. They met at a practice and when the excitement wore off, Ben became confused. "What do I have left?" he said. "I've already achieved my life's goal."

Ben wasn't the only person who felt that way about Michael.

Jordan was a global phenomenon, and even his teammates were caught up in the mystique. He hated being told that he wasn't as good as Magic Johnson or Larry Bird because he hadn't won a championship yet. His drive to succeed put enormous pressure on the organization; the players felt guilty most of the time because they weren't living up to Michael's expectations.

This created an interesting challenge for me when I became head coach. Like everyone else, I marveled at what Jordan could do with a basketball. He was Michelangelo in baggy shorts. But I knew his celebrity status isolated him from his teammates and made it harder for him to become the inspiring team leader the Bulls needed to succeed. Red Holzman once told me that the true measure of a star was his ability to make the people around him look good. Jordan still needed to learn that lesson.

THE COCOON OF SUCCESS

At first Michael and I took a wait-and-see attitude toward each other. I didn't want to become too familiar with him, as other coaches had been, because I knew it would make it harder for me to win his respect. It wasn't until we won our first championship, and he could see that the changes I had implemented actually worked, that our relationship opened up and we developed a strong partnership. Michael told me that my approach to the game reminded him of his mentor, University of North Carolina coach Dean Smith, which may have something to do with why we work so well together.

From the start I told Michael that I was going to treat him like everyone else in practice; if he made a mistake, he was going to hear about it. He took it well. Being treated like one of the guys helped Michael feel more connected to the group, and vice versa. If he wanted to, he could easily set himself apart, but he isn't built that way. The practice floor is one of the few places where he can be himself, and not Michael Jordan, Superstar. "I live a whole different lifestyle than the rest of the team, and that creates separation," he says. "My job is to tie myself back to them. And to do that I have to hang with them and maintain that closeness—get to know what they like to do, tell them about what I like to do. I don't want them to feel, 'Well, he's too great. I can't be anywhere near him. I can't touch him.' "

Unfortunately, there wasn't time for Michael do that in 1995. The craziness surrounding his return gave him and his teammates little chance to interact informally with each other. Most of the players only got to see him on the basketball court. The rest of the time he was sequestered at home or in his hotel room. This feeling of isolation was exacerbated by the fact that the makeup of the team had completely changed since his departure. Scottie Pippen, B. J. Armstrong, and Will Perdue were the only players who had worked with Michael before. He had nothing more than a passing acquaintance with the rest of the team. As a result, he seemed to them like a distant figure, mysterious and larger than life.

THE ZEN OF AIR

The first time we practiced meditation, Michael thought I was joking. Midway through the session, he cocked one eye open and took a glance around the room to see if any of his teammates were actually doing it. To his surprise, many of them were.

Michael has always maintained that he didn't need any of

"that Zen stuff" because he already had a positive outlook on life. Who am I to argue? In the process of becoming a great athlete, Michael had attained a quality of mind few Zen students ever achieve. His ability to stay relaxed and intensely focused in the midst of chaos is unsurpassed. He loves being in the center of a storm. While everyone else is spinning madly out of control, he moves effortlessly across the floor, enveloped by a great stillness.

Jordan doesn't practice visualization regularly, but he often calls up images of past successes in his mind during high-pressure situations. More often than not, he'll replay the last-second shot he took to win the 1982 NCAA championship as a freshman at North Carolina. Rather than cloud his mind with negative thoughts, he says to himself, "Okay, I've been here before," then tries to relax enough to let something positive emerge. Jordan doesn't believe in trying to visualize the shot in specific detail. "I know what I want the outcome to be," he says, "but I don't try to see myself doing it beforehand. In 1982, I knew I wanted to make that shot. I didn't know where I was going to shoot it or what kind of shot I was going to take. I just believed I could do it, and I did."

Jordan's thought process in the last seconds of Game 6 in the 1993 NBA finals is typical. We were behind by 6 points, and the crowd in Phoenix was going berserk. If we lost, it meant we would have to play the seventh game in the Suns' arena—not a happy prospect. When I called a timeout to set up a play, the other players were tense and unfocused, but Michael was remarkably composed. "I could hear all the noise," he recalls, "but I was thinking, 'No matter what happens, this is only Game Six. We've still got Game Seven.' I didn't get caught up in the surrounding rigmarole. I focused on, 'Okay, we've still got a chance to win this game. All we've got to do is get some kind of roll going, and I'm the one to do that.' My focus was right there at that particular moment. But even then I was thinking that Game Seven was a possibility. So I had a cushion." Jordan emerged from the huddle and ignited the surge with a driving layup and a critical rebound that helped us to win the game—and the championship.

LAKOTA JORDAN

In my mind, Michael is the epitome of the peaceful warrior. Day in and day out, he has endured more punishment than any other player in the league, but he rarely shows any sign of anger. Once he was upended by Detroit's front line on his way to the basket and brutally slammed to the floor. It was a malicious hit that could have caused serious damage, and I expected Michael to be fuming. But he wasn't. During the timeout that followed, I asked him if he was feeling frustrated. "No," he replied with a shrug, "I know they're going to do that when I'm in there."

Michael's competitive drive is legendary. His typical *modus operandi* is to study the opposition carefully and figure out its weakest point, then go after it like a one-man demolition crew until the team crumbles. In his early years, Michael had so much energy he would try to win games singlehandedly, but often burned out by the fourth quarter. When I took over the team, I encouraged him to conserve his energy so he would be fresh when we really needed him. But getting Michael to hold back was nearly impossible. In 1991–92, he had to be carried off the court after injuring his back. He could barely walk the next day, but he refused to watch from the sidelines. He played three games in a row that way. He was in so much pain that the trainer had to help him walk from the dressing room to the court. But as soon as he hit the floor, he was transformed into another person: Air Jordan.

Michael rarely gets depressed. During the 1989 playoffs, he blew a foul shot that would have clinched the Cleveland series. Devastated by his uncharacteristic lapse, he spent the rest of the evening, according to a friend, staring blankly at his TV set. Everybody was still morose the next day when we boarded the bus for the airport, and the trip to Cleveland for the final game. At the last minute Jordan bounded on board, glowing with confidence. "Have no fear," he announced as he walked down the aisle. "We're going to win this game." The mood lifted instantly. It wasn't so much *what* he said but *how* he carried himself that made the difference. The next day he fulfilled his promise by sinking a come-from-behind shot at the buzzer to put us ahead, 101–100. Since then, that jumper has been known in Chicago simply as The Shot.

It took a long time for Michael to realize he couldn't do it all by himself. Slowly, however, as the team began to master the nuances of the system, he learned that he could trust his teammates to come through in the clutch. The turning point was a game against the Utah Jazz in 1989. Utah's John Stockton was switching off to double-team Jordan, leaving John Paxson wide open. So Michael started feeding Paxson and John scored 27 points. Michael realized that night that he wasn't the only money player on the team. It was the beginning of his transformation from a gifted solo artist into a selfless team player.

LEADING BY EXAMPLE

As our relationship grew, I began consulting with Michael more regularly to get an inside perspective on what was happening with the team. He, in turn, started to assume a broader leadership role.

Michael isn't a cheerleader. He prefers to lead with action rather than words. As he puts it, "I'd rather *see* it done than *hear* it done." But every now and then he gives the team an inspiring pep talk. As we prepared for the 1993 finals, some of the players were worried about our chances against the Suns, who had the homecourt advantage and had beaten us in Chicago during the regular season. On the flight to Phoenix for the first two games, Jordan roamed around the team jet puffing on a cigar and saying, "We've got to go there and show them what it's like to play championship basketball." The message must have gotten through. We swept the first two games.

As a rule, Michael doesn't get involved with personnel problems, primarily because he thinks it might jeopardize his role as a leader on the floor. He doesn't want to appear too closely aligned with the coaching staff. Sometimes he needs to exploit the tension between the coaches and the players to maintain control on court.

One player he did take an active interest in was Scott Williams. When Scott was a rookie, he felt unappreciated because he wasn't getting paid much and I frequently criticized his performance. Once toward the end of the season, I took him out of a game after a few minutes because he didn't seem focused, and he started grumbling on the bench. I asked him what his problem was, and he said he needed five more rebounds to reach the bonus in his contract. (As a rule, I'm not interested in knowing that kind of information because I don't want it to influence my coaching decisions.) "Don't worry, I'll get you in in the second half," I replied. "Just don't let your mood affect the team right now." Scott went in later and made his bonus.

Jordan took Scott under his wing and showed him how to be a pro. Sometimes he would use me as a foil in his attempts to bolster Scott's ego. He'd tell Scott: "Once you're on the basketball court, don't think about Phil. Think about your team. Think about your responsibility. Phil can't play. You've got to play, and we've got to help you play." Michael wasn't always diplomatic. When Scott tried to overreach, Michael would get in his face and curse. "You're not out here to shoot," he'd start screaming. "Get back to the basics. Play defense, rebound the ball, and, when you get your opportunity to score, then you can shoot. But don't come out here and try to live up to what your friends back home feel you should be doing. Because it's not going to help us win this game." Thanks in large part to Michael's tutelage, Scott settled down and matured as an athlete and a team player.

THE STING OF FAME

An important aspect of Jordan's leadership is his handling of the media. He has never really liked working with the press, but he's skilled at dealing with reporters and takes his responsibility seriously. He started to get disenchanted with the media during the 1993 playoffs when reports surfaced that he had bet huge sums of money on golf. The stories forced the NBA to launch an investigation, which it later dropped.

Jordan was stunned at the lengths the media went to probe

into his personal life. Those feelings came up again that year when his father was murdered in South Carolina. "The only insecurity I have is with the media," he says. "Because a misinterpretation by the media is *never* corrected. They'll misinterpret a quote and say, 'I'm sorry.' But what about the people who read it? That's the power of the media today. It builds you up to the point where you're afraid to make a mistake. You're afraid to do the easiest things that could be misconstrued as negative—like going to a casino, which is very normal, very harmless, or losing money in one-on-one betting."

In the early days, Michael had a hard time saying no to reporters. The world at large expected him to be Joe All-American, and he was reluctant to disabuse anyone of that notion, even though he knew it was a fiction. *The Jordan Rules*, which came out in 1991, presented an equally distorted portrait of Michael as a sarcastic, mean-spirited egoist who spent most of his time poking fun at his teammates and Jerry Krause. Michael was furious when it appeared, but in a strange way, it had a liberating effect on him. He realized that he didn't have to be Mr. Perfect all the time, and that freed him to find out who he really was.

Now Michael has a more detached view of the press. "The media helps you become famous," he says, "but after you reach a certain level, they break you down bit by bit. It's a contradiction. If you want me to be a role model, why are you looking for negative things in my life to attack? My real job comes as soon as I step off the court and have to deal with the expectations and contradictions that come with being in the spotlight."

THE LONG GOODBYE

Michael always said that when basketball stopped being fun, he was going to walk away. During the 1992–93 season, I could see the toll the long season was taking on him. He'd always been able to bounce back quickly, but every now and then I detected an unusual bout of despondency. He'd been dropping hints all season that he might retire early, and that summer when I heard the news on the radio that his father had been murdered, my first thought was that he wouldn't be coming back for the next season.

When we finally met to talk about his decision to leave the sport in late September, Michael had thought it through from every angle. I tried to appeal to his spiritual side. I told him that God had given him a talent that made people happy, and I didn't think it was right for him to walk away. He talked about impermanence. "For some reason," he said, "God is telling me to move on, and I must move on. People have to learn that nothing lasts forever."

Then he posed an unsolvable riddle. "Can you think of any way I can just play in the playoffs?" he asked. I suggested making him a parttime player during the regular season as we had done with Cartwright the year before. He shook his head. "I'm not going to come back and play thirteen games and get criticized by the press for being a prima donna. That would be too much of a headache." I told him I couldn't think of anything else. "That answers my question," he said. "Until we can come up with a solution for that one, I must retire." (Little did I know how prophetic that conversation would be.)

Everyone expected me to be shattered by the news, but I felt surprisingly calm. My wife thought I was in a state of denial. "How do you feel, Phil?" she asked. "Are you mad at M.J.? Are you sad?" Though I wasn't happy about the news, I wasn't in a state of shock, either. Ever since his father's death, I had a strong intuition that he would be leaving the team.

What made the transition easier for me was the meeting we had with Michael in the Berto Center just before he made his official announcement to the press. I was impressed by the players' depth of feeling for Michael. We went around the room, and each one of the players made a heartfelt statement. Scottie Pippen thanked him for showing him the way, and John Paxson acknowledged how grateful he was to have played by his side. B. J. Armstrong, Jordan's closest friend on the team, said he was worried for him because now he would have "the two scariest things in life: a lot of money and a lot of free time." The person who surprised Michael the most was Toni Kukoc, who was so upset by Jordan's departure, he broke into tears.

Afterwards, the players followed Michael down to the press conference and stood by the podium while he announced his retirement. "That was true respect," Jordan recalls, deeply moved. "They didn't have to be there. They didn't have to show tears. You can't make those things up. I think it sealed the relationship between us."

About a month later, just before the season was about to start, I got a call from Michael asking if he could come down to the training center and work out with the team. He said he just wanted to check it out one more time.

It was an interesting moment. I thought he'd spend the time doing what he often did: wowing us with his one-on-one moves.

But instead, he played it straight, performing all the drills by the book. Then he walked off the court and was gone.

Later I learned that he was meeting with Jerry Reinsdorf that day to sign his letter of intent to retire. Before he did that, he needed to know if he could really leave the game behind. The answer that day was yes.

YOU CAN'T STEP IN THE

SAME RIVER TWICE

PLAYER: *So what does all this being in the moment stuff, all this jabberwocky about compassion, have to do with real life?*

ZEN COACH: *Can bulls walk on air?*

PLAYER: *Is that a koan?*

ZEN COACH: *You figure it out.*

In his book, *Thoughts Without a Thinker*, psychiatrist Mark Epstein describes an encounter in a Laotian forest monastery with a famous master, Achaan Chaa, which made an indelible impression on a group of American travelers.

"You see this goblet?" Chaa asked, holding up a glass. "For me, this glass is already broken. I enjoy it; I drink out of it. It holds my water admirably, sometimes even reflecting the sun in beautiful patterns. If I should tap it, it has a lovely ring to it. But when I put this glass on a shelf and the wind knocks it over or my elbow brushes it off the table and it falls to the ground and shatters, I say, 'Of course.' When I understand that this glass is already broken, every moment with it is precious."

In its simplicity this story illustrates one of the basic principles of Buddhist teachings: that impermanence is a fundamental fact of life. So it is, the tale seems to be saying, for everything from crystal goblets to championship basketball teams.

It wasn't until Michael Jordan left the Bulls in the fall of 1993 that I began to see what we'd really accomplished and how all the pieces of our crazy-quilt style of coaching fit together. It was a new season, and though many of the players remained, it was a new team. The challenge was not to try to repeat ourselves but to use what we had learned to re-create ourselves—to conjure up a new vision for *this* team.

Basketball had taught me many lessons about impermanence and change. I was about to learn another one.

TRANSITION GAME

In the weeks following Jordan's retirement, an eerie gloom hovered over the team. The day after the news broke, the Las Vegas line on the Bulls winning a fourth championship dropped from 1 in 5 to 1 in 24. Some insiders were even more pessimistic. One of our pr guys confessed to me that he picked the team to finish 27–55 in the office pool.

I was more sanguine. When a star of Jordan's caliber retires, there's usually a dropoff of fifteen games or more. I didn't think the Bulls would sink that far, but I was concerned about how the players would respond to the loss. My hope was that once the initial shock wore off, the veterans who had been playing in

Jordan's shadow for so long would seize the opportunity to prove to the world that they could win a championship on their own.

Losing Michael presented a major challenge for me, though not an entirely unwelcome one. What's exciting about coaching is the building process, not the ongoing maintenance work required once your team has achieved success. During Michael's final season, the Bulls ran pretty much on automatic. The biggest problem I faced was keeping the players from getting bored and losing their edge. Now I would get a chance to reshape the team and see if our approach to the game would work without the world's greatest player on the roster.

Not that there weren't problems. At the start of the 1993–94 season, we had four veterans recovering from injuries: Pippen, Cartwright, Paxson, and Scott Williams. Also, the timing of Jordan's announcement—a few days before the start of training camp—made it difficult for Jerry Krause to find a replacement for him. All of the top free agents were gone, so Krause turned to Pete Myers, a veteran who had once played for the Bulls and was eager to get back to the NBA after spending a year in the Italian pro league. The team Krause put together was a patchwork blend of insiders and outsiders, champions and nonchampions, haves and have-nots. Many of the free agents were getting rock-bottom salaries, between $150,000 to $200,000 a year, while most of the veterans were multimillionaires.

REBUILDING

The free agents' hunger helped energize the team, but it was difficult blending such a diverse group into a harmonious unit.

The players weren't in each other's blood the way the members of the earlier teams had been, and it often showed on court. One of the first things I noticed was that everyone was trying to fill the Jordan vacuum singlehandedly. All of a sudden, several players started to compete to see who could become "The Man." I had to remind them that it wasn't Jordan's team or any other individual's team, for that matter; it was *our* team. As long as they vied for the spotlight, the players would have difficulty finding a new identity as a group.

For Toni Kukoc, being "The Man" was second nature. He'd been the star on every team he'd ever played for and had developed a lot of bad habits along the way. It was obvious what Toni's agenda was: every time he got the ball, he wanted to do something special with it. This drove the rest of the players crazy. They'd expect him to do one thing, then all of a sudden he'd start freelancing and throw everybody else off. Theoretically, the other players should have been able to adjust, but Toni's playful meanderings around the court often defied logic.

Toni wasn't a selfish player. Nothing gave him more pleasure than to dish the ball off to somebody else. But he didn't want to conform to the triangle offense. I knew right from the start that I would have to ride him hard in practice to protect him from being torn apart by his teammates. I'm sure my method didn't seem like an act of kindness to Toni. He couldn't understand why I allowed Scottie the freedom to make creative moves outside the system, but would start yelling at him when he tried similar gambits. The difference, I told him, was that Scottie was looking at the game from a completely different perspective. He had spent years working within the offense, so when he decided to step outside of it, he usually had a good reason. But when Toni bucked the system, it was because he was impatient and wanted to assert his individuality, often at the team's expense.

Kukoc wasn't the only player having a hard time. Horace Grant and Scott Williams, who were playing out their options that year, had distanced themselves from the team, and Corie Blount, a rookie power forward, felt like an outsider. In February the team started to flounder, and I called a meeting to discuss the lack of cohesiveness. Afterwards, assistant coach Jim Cleamons gave the players a short, but moving speech. "We've always been a team that played from the heart," he said. "But we've gotten away from that. We're thinking about money; we're thinking about our careers; we're thinking about our stats, instead of thinking about our teammates and how we're going to get ourselves into the game."

Inspired by Cleamons' words, the players had one of their best practices of the season that afternoon. Horace and Scott recommitted their energy, and the Bulls soon became a team again. We went on a 17–3 streak in March and April and came within two games of finishing first in the conference. We rode that momentum into the first round of the playoffs and swept Cleveland in three games. Then we headed to New York for the Eastern semifinals.

1.8 SECONDS THAT SHOOK THE WORLD

This series was the most memorable clash ever between the two teams. After we dropped a 15-point lead and lost the first game, my strategy was to do an end-around on the New York media, but the reporters were craftier than I imagined. We were scheduled to practice the next day at an athletic club near Wall Street. I thought it would be unproductive for the players to spend the morning being grilled by reporters and rehashing a tough loss. So as we approached the gym, I told the bus driver to take us to the Staten Island Ferry. Little did I know that a pack of reporters had been tailing us from the hotel and were ready and waiting, notebooks in hand, when we lined up for the boat.

That wasn't our first impromptu field trip. I like to do the unpredictable every now and then to keep the players from getting stale. In 1993, for example, I canceled a shootaround in Washington, D.C., to take them to visit Bill Bradley in the U.S. Senate. The Staten Island trip was a little more leisurely. It was a perfect spring day, and we had the top deck of the boat all to ourselves. Scott Williams later told a reporter he found the trip mentally refreshing: "We came away saying, yeah, we blew one, but let's forget about it and come back with a good mental attitude."

The team played with renewed energy the next day, but the Knicks beat us again in the fourth quarter. That set the stage for one of the most surrealistic events I've ever seen on a basketball court: Game 3 in Chicago.

The weirdness began to build in the second quarter when a fight broke out between backup guard Jo Jo English and the Knicks' point guard Derek Harper that spilled into the stands a few rows down from where NBA Commissioner David Stern was sitting. Both English and Harper were ejected, and the Knicks started to fall apart, but they climbed back in the fourth quarter and tied the score with 1.8 seconds left. I called time out and drew up a play that called for Pippen to pass the ball inbounds to Kukoc for the final shot. Breaking out of the huddle, I heard Scottie grumble "bullshit." He was already angry at Kukoc for creating a traffic jam on the previous play and forcing him to take a bad shot. Now Toni was getting a chance to be "The Man."

I told Scottie what had happened on the previous play didn't matter anymore. "You had an opportunity to score, and it didn't work," I said. "Now we're going to do something else." Then I turned around, assuming the problem had been solved. But a few seconds later I glanced over my shoulder and saw Scottie hunched over at the far end of the bench, glowering.

"Are you in or out?" I asked him, puzzled by his behavior.

"I'm out," he said.

His reply caught me off guard, but I didn't have time to argue. I called another timeout and replaced Scottie with Pete Myers, one of our better passers. Myers lofted a perfect pass to Kukoc, and Toni tossed in the game-winning shot at the buzzer. Pippen just sat there and watched.

I felt sorry for Scottie as I walked off the court and made my way to the dressing room. I knew the fallout from this incident would haunt him for days, if not the rest of his career. He had broken one of the unspoken rules of sports, and I wasn't sure if his teammates, not to mention the media, would ever forgive him. Despite his reputation as a malcontent, I couldn't remember Scottie ever challenging one of my decisions. He was one of the most selfless players on the team. That's why I had named him a cocaptain with Bill Cartwright after Michael retired. But none of that mattered now. In a rash moment, he had violated the trust of his teammates.

My guess was that frustration had blurred Scottie's thinking. And I knew that if I came down too hard on him, it would only make matters worse. Scottie is a brooder. When things go wrong for him, he often falls into a deep funk that lasts for days. I knew the incident would weigh on his mind like a Sisyphean boulder.

All these thoughts were buzzing around in my mind as I stood over a sink in the shower room, taking out my contact lenses and preparing to talk to the team. Just then I heard Cartwright gasping for air in the showers. He was so overcome with emotion he could barely breathe.

"What's wrong, Bill?" I asked.

"I can't believe what Scottie did," he said in a faint whisper. "I've got to say something."

By then, all the players had returned to the dressing room except Kukoc, who was doing a TV interview. The room, in the nether region of Chicago Stadium, was cramped, poorly lit, and smelled like an old, forgotten gym bag. Its dank cavelike atmosphere heightened the feeling of intimacy.

After I made a few remarks, Bill took over. "Look, Scottie," he said, staring at Pippen, "that was bullshit. After all we've been through on this team. This is our chance to do it on our own, without Michael, and you blow it with your selfishness. I've never been so disappointed in my whole life."

When he finished, tears were streaming down his cheeks. The room was silent. Bill is a proud, stoic man who commanded the highest respect because of his ability to endure punishment and not back down. None of us had ever seen him show the slightest hint of vulnerability. In fact, his wife, Sheri, later told June that in fifteen years of marriage, she had never seen Bill cry. For him to break down like that in front of his teammates was significant, and Pippen knew that as well as anyone.

After Bill's speech I led the group in the Lord's Prayer, then left for the press conference. The players continued to meet in private. Visibly shaken by Bill's words, Scottie apologized to his teammates, explaining the frustration he felt during the final minutes. Then some of the other players said what they felt. "I've been to that point," says B. J. Armstrong. "I know what it's like to be so angry you want to quit. But to quit at that moment, especially on John Paxson and Bill Cartwright, was not right. I felt strongly about that. John was going to retire at the end of the season, and Bill was on his last go-round with the team. We owed it to them to get out there no matter what." Talking it through helped repair the broken circle. "To be honest," adds B. J., "I think the whole thing brought us closer. Because we weren't going to let one incident, no matter how big or small, break down what we had worked so hard to build."

The next morning Pippen told me he had worked everything out with his teammates. He assured me that he'd be in the right state of mind for the next game. Watching him hustle for the ball at practice, I could see that the boulder had been lifted from his shoulders.

After the dust had settled, several friends told me that they admired the way I handled the situation. But really all I did was to step back and let the team come up with its own solution.

TURNING POINT

That was a turning point for the Bulls. In the process of healing the wound, the players had found a new identity for the team *sans* Michael Jordan, and they played with a poise and self-assurance I hadn't seen since the 1993 playoffs. The story has a strange twist, though. We dominated the Knicks in the next three games, but a controversial call on Pippen with three seconds left erased our one-point lead in Game 5. The law of basketball karma, it seems, finally caught up with Scottie and ultimately the Bulls. As a result, we lost to the Knicks in seven games, instead of beating them in six. If it hadn't been for that call, we might have won our fourth championship in a row.

That was my favorite season that we didn't come away with a trophy. I was pleased with the way the players had transcended the loss of Jordan and turned themselves into a real team. Three championships had taught them a lot. On paper they may not have been as talented as their rivals, but they had an unshakable collective will that won them a lot of close games. Players like Pippen, Cartwright, Grant, and Paxson couldn't bear the idea of lapsing into mediocrity. They expected to win the big ones, even when they were outgunned, and that alone often carried them to victory.

I realized that the new team would take time to evolve into a cohesive whole. My challenge was to be patient. There's no percentage in trying to push the river or speed up the harvest. The farmer who's so eager to help his crops grow that he slips out at night and tugs on the shoots inevitably ends up going hungry.

THE TRUTH OF TRANSIENCY

In *Zen Mind, Beginner's Mind*, Suzuki Roshi writes that when we "cannot accept the truth of transiency, we suffer." I had to remind myself of this again and again at the start of the 1994–95 season. Over the summer I had watched the team I had worked so hard to build dissolve in front of my eyes. First, John Paxson retired. Then Scott Williams and Horace Grant signed free-agent deals with Philadelphia and Orlando, respectively, and Bill Cartwright, on the verge of retirement, signed with Seattle. The loss of Horace was especially painful. At one point during the negotiations, Horace reached a verbal agreement with Jerry Reinsdorf to stay with the Bulls, but he backed out of the deal after discussing it with his agent. I've never talked to Horace about why he changed his mind, but I suspect he felt he needed to go somewhere else to grow psychologically and be treated as a seasoned veteran. No matter how much money we paid him in Chicago, he might have always felt like the class dunce.

At one point, it looked as though we might lose Pippen, too. The Seattle Supersonics offered to trade us All-Star power forward Shawn Kemp, guard Rickey Pierce, and a draft pick for Pippen, but the deal fell through at the last minute. Scottie, who was already upset about being underpaid compared to other NBA stars, felt that Jerry Krause had misled him about what was going on. In January he asked to be traded, hoping that a new club would tear up his contract and pay him what he thought he was worth. He was quoted as saying he would go anywhere, even to the lowly Los Angeles Clippers.

Luckily, Pippen's dispute with management didn't affect his performance on court; in fact, he was having the best season of his career. But the team was inconsistent, and I started getting concerned about our inability to finish games. We were falling apart in the closing minutes and losing to teams we should have beaten—Washington, New Jersey, and even, God forbid, the Clippers. February was the cruelest month. We played eight of our thirteen games on the road and won only two of them. Scottie thought the problem was that the players were sitting back and waiting for him to perform a miracle, just as they had done with Michael Jordan before him. My reading of the situation was that, as a group, the team didn't have an overwhelming desire to win. And that's something you just can't teach.

Then Jordan returned.

Michael had enough competitive drive for twelve men, and I was certain some of it would inevitably rub off on the rest of the team. But in the back of my mind, doubts lingered. After his 55-point extravaganza in New York, Michael settled down and focused on working within the offense. But the team often flowed better when he wasn't on the floor, and Michael was still groping around trying to figure out his teammates. By the time we polished off Charlotte, 3–1, in the first round of the playoffs, the team had become overly dependent on him, especially in the fourth quarter. I could sense that the other players had lost some of their confidence: they felt that Michael was going to have to score 35 to 40 points a game for us to beat our next opponent— the Orlando Magic.

DOWN AND OUT IN DISNEY WORLD

Our plan was to keep the ball out of Shaquille O'Neal's hands and prevent Orlando's three-point shooters, Anfernee Hardaway, Nick Anderson, and Dennis Scott, from taking over. To contain Shaq, a 7'1", 301-pound force of nature, we unleashed the Three-Headed Monster, centers Luc Longley, Will Perdue, and Bill Wennington. That strategy worked in Game 1, but Michael squandered a one-point lead in the last ten seconds, making two surprising mental errors.

In the locker room, I put my arm around Michael and told him to forget what had happened. But I could tell by his expression that he wasn't going to let himself off that easily. The next day Nick Anderson, who had stolen the ball away from Michael to spark Orlando's go-ahead basket, was quoted in the papers, saying:

"Before [Jordan] retired, he had that quickness, explosiveness. Not that it's not there now, but it's not the same as No. 23."

When Michael showed up for Game 2, he had traded in his new number, 45, for his old one, 23. Then he proceeded to score 38 points and lead the team to a 104–94 victory. But the brouhaha that followed his number switch set Michael even further apart from the rest of the team. Orlando complained to the NBA, and so did a lot of parents who had purchased No. 45 jerseys for their kids. The league fined the Bulls $25,000, even though there was no rule prohibiting what Michael had done, and threatened to raise the stakes much higher if he didn't go back to No. 45 for Game 3. Finally, after a long, heated conference call with Michael and Jerry Krause, league officials decided to postpone any further action until after the playoffs. (Subsequently, the Bulls were fined $100,000 for their noncompliance with the league's rules. That amount will probably be lessened through negotiation.)

We split the next two games in Chicago and returned to Orlando for the critical Game 5. In the first half, it looked like we might walk away with the game, but the Magic roared back in the third quarter and won, 103–95, led by none other than Horace Grant, who went 10 for 13 from the field and scored 24 points. The next day Jerry Krause, who had been taking a lot of heat for letting Grant go, pleaded with me: "Can't you find somebody else other than Horace to beat us?"

Actually, Horace wasn't the problem. Time was. By Game 6 it was clear that this version of the Bulls didn't have the deep intuitive knowledge of each other that a team needs to work harmoniously under pressure, and which takes years to develop. This club didn't have the same "think power," to use Michael's phrase, that the championship Bulls teams had. Everybody was relying heavily on Michael, but he didn't know his teammates well enough to be able to anticipate how they would respond during crunch time. And they were in the dark about him.

This became glaringly apparent in the last three minutes of the game. B. J. Armstrong put us ahead by 8 points with a 3-pointer from the corner, and I told the players to slow things down and try to maintain control of the tempo. But they were out of sync, and Orlando stole back the momentum. In our final seven possessions, nobody scored. Kukoc tried. Pippen tried. Jordan tried. Longley tried with two players hanging on his arms. But it was not to be.

After the game, I felt stunned. The end had come crashing down so suddenly. I tried to lift the players' spirits, recounting the steps we had taken since the start of the season. "Just swallow this loss and digest it," I said. "Then get on with your lives." On the drive home, June and I talked about the season and what an emotional ride it had been. As we pulled away from the United Center and headed for the expressway, she started to cry.

THE FOOTFALL OF IMPERMANENCE

The best part of winning, I once heard someone say, is that it's not losing. There's something to be said for that. Losing can open the lid on a Pandora's box of dark emotions. Some coaches go home after big losses and start smashing up the furniture or browbeating their kids. Others put their energy into complaining about the referees or tyrannizing their players. My method is to direct my anger at a much easier target—myself.

That night I woke up at about four in the morning obsessing

about a call on Scottie Pippen at the end of the game. My mind was running wild, replaying the last three minutes over and over. What could I have done differently? What was our fatal flaw? When I was a player, I used to torture myself after games, reliving all my mistakes in the movie house of my mind. Now I'm more compassionate toward myself, but the images keep fast-forwarding through my head just the same.

In 1994 I was too shaken by our loss to New York in Game 7 of the Eastern Conference semifinals to study the tape afterwards, and memories of the game haunted me all summer. That was a hard moment for me—the first time we had been knocked out of the playoffs in four years. After the buzzer sounded, I headed toward the Knicks' bench to shake hands with Pat Riley, but by the time I made my way through the crowd he was already gone. The whole experience left a bad taste in my mouth.

This time I was determined not to dance away from reality, but to make it my teacher. Losing is a lens through which you can see yourself more clearly and experience in the blood and the bones the transient nature of life. The day after the final game, the coaches and I got together at the Berto Center and did a postmortem. Then over the next few days, Jerry Krause and I met with each player individually to discuss the season and see how they were handling the loss. As we talked, a vision of the future started forming in my mind. I could imagine a new incarnation of the Bulls built around the new Michael Jordan, now an elder statesman, not a young rambunctious warrior.

That week, my assistant, Pam Lunsford, handed me a letter from a fan in Massapequa, New York, that put our loss to the Magic in perspective:

Dear Mr. Jackson,

I just had to write to tell you how much I enjoy watching the Bulls play. You have such an exciting team with so much talent.

I must admit I only became interested in basketball a few years ago, primarily because of Michael Jordan, but as I continued to watch the Bulls in action, I became a real fan! I don't know how men view sports, but, as a woman, I appreciate it when there is mutual respect among the players and a real team effort. From what I can see, the Bulls are not arrogant and do not mouth off. They act very professionally when they are on court. Even when they are called for a foul, they don't throw temper tantrums.

I realize the team will probably never get to read my letter, but I would appreciate it if you would pass along my comments to them, just to encourage them. Let them know I don't only admire them for their talent, but respect each one because of their attitude.

Sincerely yours,
Lillian Pietri

We must be doing something right. Despite the unpredictable nature of the game, our way of working offers a genuine center, a still point in a sea of change. The makeup of the team might be different from year to year, but the principles of selflessness and compassion that guided the Bulls to three straight championships will always be available to us.

THE JOURNEYWORK OF STARS

June gets frustrated by how little emotion I display after big victories. Once she suggested that I wave to her in the stands after games "to let me know how happy you are about winning." Although I'm not demonstrative by nature, recently I've begun to take her up on her request.

Winning is important to me, but what brings me real joy is the experience of being fully engaged in whatever I'm doing. I get unhappy when my mind begins to wander, during wins as well as losses. Sometimes a well-played defeat will make me feel better than a victory in which the team doesn't feel especially connected.

This hasn't always been the case. As a young player, winning meant everything to me. My sense of self-worth rose and fell depending on my personal performance and how my team stacked up. In 1978, my last year with the Knicks, we were swept by Philadelphia in the playoffs. After the next-to-last game, Doug Collins, then a player with the 76ers, came over to shake my hand, but I snubbed him. June, who was watching from the stands, couldn't believe her eyes. I explained that the series wasn't over yet, and I wasn't prepared to acknowledge defeat. She thought that was ridiculous. Doug wasn't trying to one-up me; he just wanted to congratulate me for a good game.

She was right. My obsession with winning had robbed me of my joy in the dance. From that point on, I started looking at competition differently. I realized that I'd been trapped for years on an emotional roller coaster of winning and losing, and it was tearing me apart.

I wasn't alone. Our whole social structure is built around

rewarding winners, at the perilous expense of forsaking community and compassion. The conditioning starts early, especially among boys, and never stops. "There is no room for second place," the late coach Vince Lombardi once said. "It is and always has been an American zeal to be first in anything we do, and to win and to win and to win." How can anyone, from sports figures to entrepreneurs, possibly maintain their self-esteem when this attitude dominates our cultural mindset?

Eventually, everybody loses, ages, changes. And small triumphs—a great play, a moment of true sportsmanship—count, even though you may not win the game. Walt Whitman got it right when he wrote, "I believe a leaf of grass is no less than the journey-work of the stars." As strange as it may seem, being able to accept change or defeat with equanimity gives you the freedom to go out on the floor and give the game your all.

I used to believe that the day I could accept defeat was the day I would have to give up my job. But losing is as integral a part of the dance as winning. Buddhism teaches us that by accepting death, you discover life. Similarly, only by acknowledging the possibility of defeat can you fully experience the joy of competition. Our culture would have us believe that being able to accept loss is tantamount to setting yourself up to lose. But not everyone can win all the time; obsessing about winning adds an unnecessary layer of pressure that constricts body and spirit and, ultimately, robs you of the freedom to do your best.

When I learned to shift my focus—two steps forward, one step back—from winning and losing to my love of the game, the sting of defeat began to diminish. Once, after a game in Denver, my sister-in-law dropped by the locker room and told me that she'd broken into tears watching me coach. "I started crying," she said, "because I realized that this is exactly what you were meant to do. You're so comfortable out there. It just seems so right."

That's when I come alive: on the basketball court. As the game unfolds, time slows down and I experience the blissful feeling of being totally engaged in the action. One moment I may crack a joke and the next cast a woeful look at a ref. But all the while I'm thinking: how many timeouts do we have left? Who needs to get going out there on court? What's up with my guys on the bench? My mind is completely focused on the goal, but with a sense of openness and joy.

In its own way, basketball is a circus. When the tension builds, I'll often call a timeout to slow the game down and plan our next move. The players will be wiped out, anxiously trying to pull themselves together before they have to make their next run. And after they've taken a drink and settled into their chairs, what do they see out on the court? Young women waving pompoms. Children racing around the floor in go-carts. Grown men in gorilla suits trying to slam dunk a ball from a trampoline.

That's when you realize that basketball is a game, a journey, a dance—not a fight to the death.

It's life just as it is.

ACKNOWLEDGMENTS

We owe a special debt of gratitude to Lynn Nesbit, warrior agent, for finding the right home for *Sacred Hoops*. We are also deeply grateful to Todd Musburger, John M. Delehanty, and Bennett Ashley for their inspired teamwork and undying faith in the project.

Thanks to Bob Miller and Leslie Wells at Hyperion for recognizing what this book could become and helping us bring it to fruition.

Thanks to Helen Tworkov and Carole Tonkinson at *Tricycle: The Buddhist Review* for putting us together and planting the seed for the book in our minds.

Thanks to Pam Lunsford for her dedication and hard work; to Tex Winter for his basketball genius; to B. J. Armstrong, Bill Cartwright, Jim Cleamons, Craig Hodges, Michael Jordan, Jerry Krause, and John Paxson for their insights; and to Tim Hallam and Tom Smithburg for a team effort beyond the call of duty.

We are also indebted to Landon Y. Jones for his support and encouragement; to Amy Hertz for nurturing the book from the start; and to Dan Wakefield and Steven Winn for their perceptive reading of the manuscript. In addition, we would like to thank the following for their invaluable contributions: Richard Baker, Charlotte Joko Beck, Anna Christensen, Eugene Corey, John J. Delehanty, Mark Epstein, Elise Frick, Mike Her Many Horses, Melissa Isaacson, Charles and Joe Jackson, Sheldon Lewis, Ted Panken, John Sloss, Paul Weinberg, Martha White, Workman Publishing, and, last but not least, the Empress of Blandings.

Finally, we would like to thank our children, Elizabeth, Chelsea, Brooke, Charley and Ben Jackson, and Clay McLachlan, for teaching us spiritual lessons that could never be learned from a book.